Candelabracadabra

Scott Belden

Cover art: germancreative - Lesia

Printed in the United States of America
First printing, 2023
ISBN 979-8-218-25765-1

Candelabracadabra

Names have been changed.

Lunch

Senior year of high school, I was relegated to a different lunch shift than that of my friends, whom I had eaten with for the previous five years. Worried of being seen eating alone in the cafeteria, I opted for the safer and equally uncomfortable decision to drive off and eat in my car. This worked most days, except for the day I forgot to close my trunk, and it bounced up and down as I exited the parking lot, never latching, and drawing the attention of everyone I passed by.

For the first months of senior year, I would drive out to the nearby Phillips 66 and park next to the side of the building. The gas station was just far enough away to eat up the time of the lunch hour, the time I didn't need to buy a bottle of cranberry juice and digest a mediocre sandwich.

One sunny day, as I was walking out to my car for lunch as usual, I noticed James, easily identified by his braids, standing with a friend facing the parking lot, scanning for someone they could ride to lunch with. I knew James from the previous summer of skateboarding, giving him rides home from the skatepark, and going on street skating trips. I met him first as a friend of my younger brother, and because of that, I always had a hard time confidently considering him a friend of my own. Apparently, he could sense this in me, as he asked me one day on the way home from the skatepark.

"Am I your friend?" James asked.

"What do you mean?" I asked, worried at the implications of my answer.

"Like, if I died would you go to my funeral?" I found this to be a curious stipulation for friendship, but I was glad to be given criteria. If that was what it meant to be a friend, then "Yeah, I'd go to your funeral."

So at lunch, I walked past James and his friend, who I would come to know as Donald, knowing that James would probably call out to me, but still waiting for him to initiate it.

"Scott!" he said, "are you going to lunch?

"Yep."

"Can we ride with you?"

I smiled and nodded, put some breath into "sure." For some reason, I was afraid to speak to others across distances in a large open space, especially when I knew that many of my classmates were nearby. I continued walking toward my car, looking back just enough to notice James and Donald look at each other, like "are you thinking what I'm thinking." They jogged after me, holding their books in one arm and the waist of their pants up with the other.

For the previous months of going to my car for lunch, I was always self-conscious, paranoid of people watching me, being alone. That day, as I pulled out the keys to unlock the Honda, I still felt conscious of others seeing me, but today, instead of being seen as alone, I was conscious of being seen with two black kids waiting to get into the car as well. Asking James where he wanted to go to lunch, I put my backpack into the trunk and avoided eye contact with any neighboring drivers.

As I got in the driver's seat and James settled in to shotgun, I started to feel comfort coming back. All of a sudden, the Honda Accord had been transformed back into the good times of the summer: James dominating the radio, overriding my pleas to turn down the bass on the way to the skate spot. As I backed out and headed toward the exit of the parking lot, James spotted some of his friends and told me to stop for a second. A group of at least five of his friends wanted to ride along, but Dante and Trevyon beat everyone to the last two seats in the back, and pushed the car to its maximum capacity. Not just that all the seatbelts were taken, but that Donald, Dante and Trevyon were crammed in the back and literally pressed up against the windows. This provided for the funniest exchange of insults I had heard in a while.

"Dang, fat nose! Make the whole car sink down!"

"Shut up, y'ol' biscuit mouth."

"Turtle mouth."

"Bean face."

"Gravy neck."

James had pioneered a system of insults, the standard formula involving an extraneous object tied to a body part. "Turtle, frog, and biscuit" were the most common objects, and "nose, neck and mouth" were the go-to body parts. Creativity was the goal; therefore, "turtleneck" was never an accepted combination.

In the turn lane to exit the parking lot, James suggested some beats to accentuate what had instantly become a good time. I even pulled out my Bono shaded sunglasses for some flair. After scanning my collection, James resorted to a CD from Dante, a burned copy of Fat Tone's *Tha Stick Up Kid*. At the time, I knew nothing of Fat Tone. Now, I

9

know all I need to know about him. For example, the track listings of the CD include "We G's" and "We Gangsta," back to back. We decided to drive out to my house during lunch, where I thought there might be more food variety for the group than the gas station. Where I could make my own lunch that I hadn't had time to prepare that morning. And, probably most important for James, the trip to my house provided the most opportunity for riding and blasting Fat Tone with the windows down and the bass up.

I suggested that we listen to something besides Fat Tone, and in rebuttal, James switched to whatever radio station I had programmed, automatically proclaimed it white music and began his impression of a white kid: eyes squinted and face in a grimace to the sound of electric guitars, exclaiming "dude" a lot. I laughed and started my defense, but realized that I wouldn't be able to get a legitimate argument out over Fat Tone.

As we got on the highway, Dante asked me if I was good at skateboarding. In jest, I answered "Not as good as James," to which he replied "Go to sleep." James was good at skateboarding, though not as devoted as the rest of us. I learned that as time went on and James became more comfortable getting rides from me, it became less important where we skated, and more important that wherever we go, we play his music of choice at his level of choice.

As we neared my house, I heard comments from the back seat about the surroundings. We passed the newly built subdivision, featuring houses in the $300,000 price range. My house was in the older part of the neighborhood farther inside, but was still large enough that I always felt guilty when people remarked that it was a big house.

"This is a *nice* neighborhood," Trevyon said.

"I bet this is the kind of neighborhood where you could leave your stuff outside wouldn't have to worry about it getting stolen," Dante added. I smiled, considering that luxury for the first time as I pulled into my driveway and pressed the garage door opener. I turned off the ignition and the radio, realizing that the sounds of Fat Tone reverberating through the neighborhood were alien to the home-schooled children across the street. I headed into the garage trying to decide what I would be able to provide for everyone to eat, while Trevyon hurried Dante out of the car so he could get out.

I examined the contents of the garage refrigerator. Assuming Tofurkey and Veggie Dogs would be unpopular, I suggested beer.

"We've got some beer. Do you guys want beer for lunch?"

"Nah, we don't drink," Dante said.

"Yeah, we do the opposite," Trevyon added, by which I assumed he meant smoking.

I led the way into the kitchen, which had been remodeled since James had last been over.

"Whoa, when did you do this?" James asked.

"A couple weeks ago," I said.

"Rich neck."

I checked the kitchen fridge while James pointed out the trampoline in the backyard to the guys.

"Whoa, I'm about to go jump on that," Dante said. I wondered what he wanted to eat for lunch, but realized that maybe food wasn't a priority for any of them. I encouraged them to go out and have at the trampoline.

Before descending the back porch, Dante asked if I had any German Shepards or anything that would attack him, and I said no. After setting foot on the stairs, he started running back into the kitchen, and I remembered Max in the backyard. Definitely not a German Shepard, nor threatening in any way, just excited as usual and running up the stairs to see who had arrived.

"I seen a dog running at me and I was like *hell no!*" Dante exclaimed. I said I was sorry and that Max wouldn't hurt him. He and the guys headed back outside while Max approached for a belly rub. After they had all headed out, I started working on my own peanut butter and jelly sandwich, then decided to get some bread and ham—actual ham— ready for the guys in case. I looked out the window and saw James bouncing high on the trampoline. The trampoline suddenly regained some purpose in our backyard. Trampolines lose their novelty after a while, and looking out the window, I saw it was rejuvenated. It surrounded by basketball jerseys and crisp white T-shirts, multi-colored fitted hats. It was like springtime for the trampoline area, while the rest of the backyard remained in fall mode.

By now, if I had any concerns, they were concerns for hospitality, and then getting back to school on time for fifth hour. Having the sandwiches and chips ready, I decided we needed to go, and the best way to get their attention was to throw a tennis ball from the deck at James. I missed, he threw it back at me, and I said we should go. However, none of us were in such a hurry to get back to the car before seeing the 220-pound Dante attempt a front flip on the trampoline. Amazingly, he pulled it off, the most impressive thing I had seen done on the trampoline.

We made our way back to the car, climbed in, with bickering over having to take the middle of the backseat, or sit next to Dante. I handed them the chips and sandwich material, closed the garage door, backed out the driveway and started back towards the school. Near the first stop sign out of the neighborhood, James stopped me from trying to eat a sandwich and drive a car full of people.

"I'm not trying to die. Lemme drive." I had let him drive a few times during the summer, sometimes because I didn't want to drive, sometimes because he and the rest of the people in the car wanted him to drive more than they wanted me to. I climbed over to the front passenger seat.

After he settled in and adjusted the seat and mirrors, I was told I was in charge of the music now.

Dante said, "Could you go to track... 14... no, 9, and turn it up please?"

I responded with "A'ight." Before I could retract it, Dante had already looked at Trevyon, and they had started cracking up. It was at first somewhat restrained, but after seeing my smile as well, they let the laughter out.

James drove us back to Hickman. Fat Tone blared once again.

Pulling back into the school parking lot, I regained a lot of self-awareness. James was driving, and he wasn't going to let an opportunity pass by for him to show off while driving the car. He opted for circling around the school's circle drive once or twice, making sure to be seen by the students outside the cafeteria. I tried to stay somewhat low, didn't really look out the window for fear of eye contact. In the parking lot, I directed James to my parking spot, and he got close enough to parking within the lines. James and his friends said thanks and then jogged off to class, for fear of the third tardy, after which came detention. I lingered at the car, getting my backpack out of the trunk, in a manner all to similar to the lunches of earlier in the year. I again wondered what people would think of me, though I had not been alone. I was nervous, but soon comforted by the call of my name.

"Scott! Come here." It was Craig, one of my friends I didn't usually see out in the parking lot, a couple spaces down climbing out of the car with Jimmy.

"Who was that riding in your car?" Craig asked me.

"James, and some of his friends," I said.

"You mean his *crew*?" Craig asked.

"No, just some of his friends." Jimmy came around from the driver's seat of his Volvo and joined the conversation.

"Yeah, I looked over there and I was like 'Who's that pimp riding with all those huge G's?'"

"Whatever, I just knew James from skating, and so he and some friends wanted to go to lunch," I said.

"Admit it, Scott," Craig said, "hanging out with black people makes you cool."

I walked with Craig and Jimmy into the school. The hallways were crowded. The foyer was a place I dreaded walking in each morning, alone, hoping no one would notice me.

"You're not cool," a girl had once said, walking next to me in the hallway, mistaking my silence and straight faced-ness for arrogance. It was simply that I was paralyzed.

Now, I ducked into the bathroom for respite, not needing to go. There were nervous tics I had developed. Stopping to drink at water fountains when I didn't need to. Coughing. Scratching the back of my head. This habitual scratching of the head had been captured on camera. For our broadcast journalism class, one of the teachers would film the route from the parking lot into the school building, up the stairs, and into the broadcast journalism room. On the day that he filmed it this year, to capture the new commons area, he also captured me, taking my time, blocking the way to the door to the classroom. I was scratching my head most of the time.

Today, if there had been a camera to film me, it would catch me exiting the bathroom, only to hear "Rich neck" as a friend, James, made his way down the hall.

Merit

I look back and wonder why I didn't get it sooner. Some things were scheduled— you get your driver's license around 15 or 16. You go to prom at 18 and graduate. You might get through college in four years, then go on to land a wife and a job. But for what I needed most, there was no guarantee of it, no schedule apparent to me. I just had to wait.

On the outside, everything was looking to be okay. We had regalia. Those in the Jewish community had phylacteries— small leather boxes filled with Scriptures, as a reminder of what God had done. We in Boy Scouts had merit badge sashes and fobs with beads from our campouts — reminders of what we had done. It was a cauldron of pride. As a child, rarely did I stand tall or look people in the eye, but a photo of me at a bridge-crossing ceremony shows me in uniform with my parents, back arched and face smug. I was making the transition from Cub Scouts to Boy Scouts. I wrote in my fifth grade writer's notebook, "I'm a Boy Scout! Yeah I get to go on campouts. Get merit badges, play dodge ball and more." I just need a broad-brimmed hat and some hiking boots and I'll be all the way in. To my mind at the time, it was not so much that I was climbing a ladder of achievements. Rather, I was simply moving on or up to what was next, joining a new community. It felt like growing.

Our Boy Scout Troop went to summer camp in Arkansas. Arnold Schwarzenegger played Mr. Freeze in the Batman movie that summer, and the Taco Bell we stopped at near the Missouri border had a life size photo of him on the door. An elderly man in a foot cast stood next to the door for a moment, "Not far off, huh?" he said, comparing himself to the boots in the image. This was a perfect opportunity for me, as a Boy Scout, to do my daily good turn and hold the door open for an elderly person. Hadn't this been the story of the Unknown Scout who helped William Boyce find his way in London in 1909? It was one of my favorite stories. The boy refused a tip, stating that he was a Boy Scout and was merely doing his good turn. It was a model I wanted to follow. In practice, I may have only smiled at the man, which might have counted as fulfilling one point of the Scout Law— to be cheerful.

Our first night at camp, Sean and I were partners for tents. They were the green canvas military issue tents that the camp provided, as opposed to the cozy nylon ones our parents bought. Lying on our cots, Sean and I noticed that the tent was full of daddy long legs spiders. They were there, just hovering above our heads.

"What should we do about it?" I asked Sean in the dark.

"I'm not sure. We could try to brush them out."

"We could pray," I offered tentatively. It was like asking a girl out, the same amount of unknowns at the response.

"Okay," he said.

"Okay," I said. We laid in silence for the next minute, presumably praying that God would remove the spiders.

"Okay," Sean said. "I prayed. Do you want to hear my prayer?"

"That's okay," I said. It felt too intimate. There are no atheists in the trenches, but they might not want to talk about all that God-stuff, just yet.

It was like we each had these rooms that we rarely visited or talked about—maybe a spare bedroom or closet —and then we were together in the same room talking about it. The room we met in was the Youth Group room at St. Andrew's Lutheran Church. It was not our church—with the exception of Mark and Sam. Rather, it was the church that hosted our Boy Scout Troop—Troop 706. In addition to our stack of merit badges, there was the opportunity to earn the God and Church medal—one more thing to pin to our shirts. So the adults coordinated with minister of the church lead us in weekly meetings to fulfill the requirements for the award. This was in addition to our Monday night troop meetings. We were returning to the church for extra credit, to go beyond and above.

There were eight of us, though it might have been twelve. Twelve disciples hanging out with their robed leader hoping for the next best thing, trying to keep up. In this case, our leader was not Jesus, but the church's minister—a woman with grey, bobbed hair who smiled a lot. She was the right person for the job, someone patient enough to shepherd a double-handful of sixth graders through the workbook.

We met in the Youth Group room, which may as well have been her office. There was a stack of books on the back shelf that made it seem like a library or a study. The room was narrow enough that we were stretched along in an elliptical shape on couches and beanbag chairs. I sat in a straight backed chair; the minister sat at her desk with her chair swiveled to face us.

"Let's get started, shall we?"

Her assistant, a high school aged boy with a dark goatee, walked into the room with a tray full of snacks— pretzels, tortilla chips and salsa and glass of Coke. As he attempted to set the tray down, the Coca-Cola spilled onto the tray and snacks.

"Shit," he said, and attempted to mop it up with paper towels. We all snickered that the minister's assistant had said "shit" in a church, in front of the minster. The minister smiled, too. We were off to a good start.

She passed out sheets for human bingo. I wrote my name on the middle square where it said "Sign your own name." I wrote it in cursive, as this was how we had learned to do signatures. In fact, I even put curly feet on the two t's, as this is how I had learned it the official way. I had gotten into the habit of writing my t's without the curly feet, but perhaps it was time that I got back in line.

Zach signed his name in the box that said "Someone who can sign Row Row Row your Boat." Erik signed the box for "Someone with braces."

Most of our first meeting was ice-breakers. When it was time to go, she had given us our first assignment. It was the first section of the student book, where they had listed the story of the prodigal son with some follow up questions.

I took my time working on these at home. Specifically, I took out my ruler to draw perfect, straight lines between the columns for Younger Son, Father, and Older Son on my wide-ruled looseleaf paper. It was the answer to question four. "Circle the words which you believe best fit each person, and tell why you circled them."

19

"Younger Son." I wrote it out on my paper and underlined it with the ruler in pen, making sure to mark directly on the blue line, leaving a space between the underlines in Younger and Son. I didn't know what drove me to be so particular with my penmanship. Dad once shared with me the adage "Cleanliness is next to godliness." It sounded wrong to me. Who dare compare themselves to God just by wiping off the countertops? But there was something in me that had a deep desire to do things perfectly. I wrote of the younger son in the parable. "Repentant: He ran away and sinned, but he was brave enough to go back and ask for forgiveness."

I knew that it was best to twist "brave" in the direction of morality. In the movies "brave" might mean taking an ax to the chest of an enemy, but I knew that the real answer had to do with being good.

"Older Son. Hard Worker: He stayed at home and worked for his dad because he thought it was the right thing to do." I wanted to put the most positive spin on things, opting not to choose the more negative words of "angry" "unforgiving" and "obeys." Even if obeying was technically the right thing to do, it was an ugly word.

We returned to the crowded room the next week. It was already becoming cozy. The snacks were brought before us, without a spill this time, and the minister asked us how we had found our homework assignment. The discussion began.

"Really, I think it was a darn shame," Erik started. "I mean, the younger son goes out and blows his dad's money on *prostitutes*. I mean, come on, *prostitutes*," he said smirking. "I really think that that's about the dirtiest thing you could *do*."

We all voiced grievances, inwardly jealous that he had gotten away with saying "prostitutes" as many times as he could. The minister indulged him, smiling.

"And that's the thing about God's grace," she said. "As amazing as it is, he is willing to welcome us back no matter how wild we've been."

We moved to an examination of our different religious traditions. Sean was technically Catholic, but his dad had permitted him to join with the rest of us for this series of meetings, with the workbook "Created by Protestant and Independent Christian Churches for Young People in Grades 6, 7, 8."

Sean spoke of the confessional, mentioning how you were in there speaking to someone, but you couldn't really see the other person. I struggled to picture it.

"Is it like in the cop shows, when they're looking into a mirror but really it's cops on the other side watching them?" I asked.

"Not exactly," Sean said. The minister smiled.

We followed her into the Lutheran church's sanctuary. We used this location for special events, such as the Courts of Honor when all the awards and rank advancements were presented. The room was a square shape, with reddish-orange carpets and wooden seats. A rectangular raised platform was centered near the back of the room, surrounded by rails for arms, and cushions for kneeling when communion would call parishioners up front.

At the entrance of the room was a stone structure holding holy water.

"We definitely don't have this at my church," I boasted. I made an effort to emphasize the disgust. My family was attending a non-denominational church at the time, that eschewed anything that seemed traditional. Thus, without having thought it through, I rejected the holy water, and lack of guitars and drums that any of my fellow God and Church award participants were accustomed to.

I am not sure how we got hardened into our traditions— or supposed lack of traditions— so quickly. I recall Zach's family making a church move, and Zach coming into 6th grade P.E. class with renewed zeal while we did our stretches.

"The King James Version, that's the only way to go," he told me out of the blue, before going on to sing some of *O Come, O Come, Emmanuel.* Was I all of a sudden someone who needed to be converted? The Jack Chick tract that he left on my desk in my room after school one day indicated that I was. When I asked him about it, he denied remembering leaving it there. Some things were going to remain unspoken, it seemed.

Like God's name. I recall standing in the woods behind my house with Zach, and saying "that's not what He wants of us."

"That's not what who wants of us?" Zach asked.

I pointed solemnly toward the sky, imagining that to say "God" would be to break a commandment.

My family became participants at the local church— even getting dressed up for photographs for the church's membership annual— but not on Sunday mornings. This was one of the perks of this church's new way of doing things. What we consumed in our household changed as well. Instead of listening to Disney songs in the van, we were now listening to Carman's *R.I.O.T.* The genre was contemporary Christian music, and the acronym of the album stood for Righteous Invasion of Truth.

Additionally, in my room instead of the sheet of baseball cards that my grandpa had purchased for me in fourth grade, above my bed hung a new poster— "Heaven, it's not just a dream." One of the cartoon images on the poster was of a young man speeding in a red convertible on streets of gold, with the license plate JCIS4ME. My younger brother Mark had one in his room full of animals and mentioning Psalm 104, speaking of all God's works. In the hallway was a poster of a baseball player swinging for the fences with Philippians 4:13 on it, "I can do all things through Christ who strengthens me."

The religiosity all came in at about the same time hormones did for me. So while I would wear a purple W.W.J.D. bracelet to school, I was also particularly interested in the sex scenes in my James Bond novels.

"What's 'jigagig'?" I asked Sean in our reading class. He glanced at the passage in my copy of *Goldfinger*.

"Sex," he said.

I didn't know what to do with it all, aside from to keep attending meetings. Sunday school on Sunday, Boy Scouts on Monday night, and the God and Church Award on Tuesdays.

Today I look back at the manila folder which holds the God and Church Award materials. The Lord's Prayer is taped to the front. My name is written in impeccable penmanship in pencil, with the "proud" *S* I used at the time, where it's almost as if the letter has a shrunken head but puffs its chest out. There is a printed handout discussing the importance of gathering together as the church. A list of local ministries, of which we visited one on a field trip— St. Francis House. An illustrated story of Thea Ronning— a missionary to China. This was the missionary I was assigned to study, but I recall almost nothing of her. I have a looseleaf sheet of paper where I have copied down some of Jesus' "I am" statements from the Gospel of John. There is a bookshelf illustration of the books of the Bible. And a handout about Talking With God.

Looking back at these documents, I wonder, how is it that so little sank in at the time? How could it be that I was ostensibly trying to follow Jesus, and yet was so full of myself?

I think what was missing, through no fault of the minister who led us, was a sense of rescue. It has been said that the bad news makes the good news better. I do not recall being warned that pride was a problem— particularly for someone like me, who thought he was good. The closest came from one comment from Sean's dad on a weekend campout. I resisted someone's help carrying a heavy box to my tent, and Sean's dad said graciously said something about pride. It stung a little, even though I didn't completely understand it. What did carrying a box have to do with pride? Was it really that bad that I refused someone's help? What else was I supposed to do? Was this simply another strange admonition from an adult— like the time a father insisted on us collecting the apple cores out of his van in a small trash bag before our week of canoeing?

In the moment of Sean's dad's comment, I sensed that I had fallen short by being good, but I didn't know what to do about it. It was along the lines of "Look out for pride" possibly with the word "soul" involved. He was not ashamed to use religious language. He loved me. I sensed that he grasped something I didn't yet. Still, I did not know what to do. The box had already been moved to my tent, and it seemed too late for me to ask for help.

In one sense, everything was already set up. We were in a merit machine. Everything in us and around us was churning, urging us on to do and do and do. It was fun going on campouts. Yet over time I prided myself on going to more campouts than others, and at the string of beads I would be able to keep on my fob on my belt. It was exciting to advance rank. But it required performance at the Boards of Review held in front of a handful of adults from the troop. I cried from pressure during each one, without fail, except for the final one for Eagle Scout Rank. Perhaps I sensed that I was exiting the system of merit.

On a Monday night in sixth grade, at the end of our God and Church sessions, I received my medal for the God and Church Award. For some reason, it was marked "Baptist." Dad explained that the non-denominational church we were attending had some baptist connection. The other scouts made fun of me for my baptist medal, and I was uneasy because I wasn't sure that that's what I wanted to be. The other Scout Troop across town at the baptist church I had once visited did not please me. I did not want to be like them, if that's what a baptist was. I had a sense that something was wrong, and I was stuck with it.

What Boy Scouts provided was a system of performance. There were the twelve points of the Scout Law, and I assumed I was living up to it. I was the performer. God was distant and to be revered, like plates in a china cabinet. There was little to no sense of God's activity— much less of me needing him to rescue me, even if with the baptist troop I had once heard them sing

"Amazing grace how sweet the sound that saved a wretch like me." I thought it was a catchy tune, but I did not yet consider myself a wretch. I had a fob full of beads and shirt full of medals, of which the God and Church medal was the latest. I attached it to my left breast pocket. Merit covered my heart.

Biology

Aside from Swimming, Intro to Art and French, it was the one class I was taking as a sophomore that wasn't honors. Biology. I had it sixth hour, right after lunch. The first day of class, I returned to the building on time to split off from my friends and wonder if I would know anyone in Biology. I recognized two people. Matt, with whom I had shared Kindergarten and second grade, as well as much of junior high school, and now AP World History and Literature as a sophomore. The other girl was a miniature version of Marilyn Monroe whom I had attended Sunday school with years ago. She had the blond hair and mole above her lip. Matt suggested that I sit next to her, but I chickened out and joined him at the table behind her in the back of the room.

The teacher introduced herself. She alerted us to her name change.

"I know it says Ms. Richmond on your schedules, but I got married over the summer so now it's Mrs. Smith." She was in her fifties.

"That had to be an arranged marriage," Matt said under his breath. We hadn't even made it through the first day and he was already taking shots on her.

Her hair was long, wavy brown, like from a 1970's album cover, only with the caveat that she was spending time on conservation projects and not in the studio. She made her way around the classroom introducing us to the emergency chemical shower and going over expectations for class behavior.

"One thing we ask is that you be respectful of the animals and specimens we may be working with. There will come units when we'll be working with deceased animals, and some students may be tempted to hold it up in the air and go 'Hey, look at me, look at me!'" She mimicked air puppetry. "But that's really not a respectful way to treat something that has been provided for us to learn from." This surprised me. I did not expect reverence to be expected from a room full of fourteen year olds.

In the coming days we were given assigned seats. The black slate tabletop always kept your handprint, making you wonder what was on your hand, and what was in the table. I remained in the back row but shared a table with a student named Jason who had attended a different junior high school. He had dark hair with gel in it. I judged him for having gel in his hair. I had drawn a black sheep on my spiral notebook, the same logo from Minor Threat and their EP "Out of step (with the world)." I thought that putting gel in ones hair was vain and "preppy," even though the categories from junior high were evaporating. People were still trying to be cool, but everything was more of a melting pot. I listened to Jason talking to students at nearby tables to get a read on him.

"I was in study hall, and the teacher told me to go ahead and do my reading assignment. When he came back to check on me at the end of the hour, he said, 'You have literally read one paragraph in the last forty minutes.'" Lethargy. It was to be commended at some level. Maybe I could appropriate it. *If he can do that little work and pass, what might that mean for how I approach this classroom?*

An early assignment had us describing the five classes of vertebrates. When I came to birds, I simply wrote, "You know what birds are." I got a four out of five on the assignment.

Part of me wondered if I should have gone for Honors Biology. I did not plan on being a doctor. If I had, I would have felt compelled to move in the honors direction as soon as possible. But after a negative experience in the ninth grade's Intro to Chemistry and Physics, I decided that science was not going to be my thing. It appeared that I was in good hands in general ed biology.

There were a handful of students who seemed to have known each other from time together at the other junior high school. I could not figure out all of the connections at first, but eventually I webbed it out in my mind. Evan was on the soccer team, but apparently was close friends with Ryan—perhaps from Catholic school years before. Chris was also on the soccer team with Evan, but also somehow knew Ryan. Kevin apparently knew Evan and Chris from the year before, but though he wore skateboarding shoes, was on the diving team. And they were all hilarious. I was eager for each class, just to listen to their interactions.

"I'm getting a visual on a paper with someone else's name on it," Ryan said, sounding like an astronaut. He was also heavily influenced by *The Big Lebowski*.

"Chris, the next time you and the family are gathered together, why don't you propose the ol' *Big Lebowski*." It was always, "the ol'." I mimicked him at home with my parents and brother, but I didn't dare rob him of his lines in class.

I sat in the back row of class next to Jason. There was a down moment in class and Matt, nearby, asked, "What would Scott be like at a party?"

In truth, I had not been to one. I had read about them in skateboard magazines, so that's what I went with, hazarding a response.

"I'd maybe get naked," I said, following the example of skateboarder Ed Templeton whom I admired.

Matt laughed. "Freedom, man," he said. "Just go with it and be free." There were a few more comments, and then Matt exhorted me, "Venture outside of your hole, Scott" as if I were a rodent we were studying in class.

I didn't know how to do this. I essentially had skateboarding, Minor Threat, and imagination. Actually verbalizing comments was slow to come.

There came a day in the genetics unit when we were given slips of PTC to taste. They came on strips of white plastic, like the disposable thermometers we would be offered in the nurse's office. Only this time, the teacher was passing it out to everyone in the class.

"Some of you will be able to taste this, and some of you won't." We all did so at approximately the same time, dropping them on top of our tongues like communion wafers.

"Ugh, this tastes like some ass!" Jamal said, standing up from his desk. An eruption of disgust came from Robert and Phil.

"If you need to get a drink, go ahead," Mrs. Smith said. A cluster of students rushed out of the classroom to the water fountain in the hallway.

"Damn it," Evan said, still sitting, thinking it unfair he was unable to taste the PTC. I was in his group and felt the same way, but I hesitated to commiserate vocally. I did not realize that shared experience was grounds for conversation, if only I would start it.

As assigned seats changed, I was brought closer into contact with Ryan and crew. I was seated right next to him, and Evan was not far away.

"So what are you going to do tonight," Ryan asked me on a Friday. By habit, I always waited for him to initiate dialogue, not realizing that I could do so myself.

"I might go downtown with a friend," I said, wanting to load the more impressive option first. "Or I've got this emulator for regular Nintendo games on my computer I might try."

"Emulator, huh?" he said. I didn't know what Ryan's evening plans were. I didn't ask. And it didn't occur to me to reciprocate and ask. A few comments later, Ryan said.

"I've got to be honest with you, you're not the most exciting guy in the world," Ryan told me. It stung a little, but it was another exhortation from a colleague, along the lines of "Venture outside of your hole." I didn't realize I was supposed to be exciting or exiting holes.

"Is that so?" I asked, wondering what words I could possibly come up with to make myself worth it, to recover for time lost.

"You've got to let 'em know what rumble and fire is in you," Ryan said.

Evan came to our table to talk to Ryan during a lab experiment. Somehow he talked Evan into showing off his bicep muscle to me.

"Are you ready for this? Are you ready for this?" Ryan asked me as Evan did windmill stretches with his right arm. "Show 'em what you got, Evan. Let him have it!"

31

"Bam!" Evan said, holding up his shirtsleeve. I was impressed, not just at his bicep muscle, but also that he was resorting to the physical to impress someone already smitten by the social.

Once during work time, Mrs. Smith quizzed Ryan on a portion of his worksheet he had not yet completed. After she walked away I gave him the answer she was looking for.

"Well, well, well. It seems we've got an answer box here. Where were you about ten seconds ago when Mrs. Smith was chewing me out?"

"She was asking you, not me," I said.

Evan came for assistance on his sheet, but more so for a chance to talk to Ryan.

"What did you get for number four?" Evan asked.

"I don't know, why don't you ask ol' AB here?"

"AB?" I asked.

"Answer Box."

"I haven't done that problem yet," I said.

"Oh hold on, I know what we have to do," Ryan said. He reached over and touched the back of my shoulder, flipping an imaginary switch."

"We've got to turn him on first," Ryan said. I smiled. I was being included in some sense, even if it was at cost to myself.

A few weeks later I was moved to the front of the class next to Evan.

"Mrs. Smith, what would you say is the god of the cell?" Evan asked her one day.

"The god of the cell? I'm not sure there's really a 'god' of the cell. If you mean the center of it, the nucleus perhaps…"

"No, I'm talking about the *god* of the cell," he said it while lighting up his eyes. He was on a pursuit of his own, like when he had taken the first few minutes of class to finish off listing the planets of the solar system.

Ryan made a few comments from the other side of the room. Mrs. Smith reprimanded him.

"Now do you mind if I continue with teaching the class?" she asked.

"By all means," Ryan said. "By all means."

There came a time where an assignment took us to the computer lab. I ended up with a computer next to Ryan and Evan.

"Scott, on a scale of one to ten, how badass would you say I am," Evan asked.

"What's your measuring stick for defining badass?" I replied. "Are we talking Ryany Ramone?"

"Who's Joey Ramone?"

"You know, from The Ramones. Punk rock. Leather jackets."

"What's he giving you? What's he giving you?" Ryan called out from the other side.

"I'd say you're a five," I told Evan.

"Harsh," he said. "Harsh."

Ryan resumed the conversation after Evan walked away. "I've got to be honest with you, AB. I think sometimes you play favorites, talking to Evan more than me."

"Sorry about that." Had he asked how funny I thought he was, he would have received a nine or ten.

I walked into class one day wearing my busted Jamie Thomas skateboard shoes. From consistent usage, the tongue padding on the left shoe was exploding out. Kevin wore Osiris shoes, another brand, which were still intact. It was busted usage that indicated someone was actually skating.

"Look at his shoes!" Kevin remarked.

"Yeah, it's from skating," I said.

"Are you good?" he asked. "Be honest."

"I'm all right," I said. Yet skating proficiency had little currency in this classroom. It was all about wit.

There came a unit where we were extracting DNA from a strawberry. As Mrs. Smith extracted the gooey material at the front of the room, Ryan let out a groan of fear.

"Ehh, I don't feel so good about this, Mrs. Smith. I don't feel like we should be playing God."

"Mrs. Smith is playing God, everybody," Evan joined in.

The next year, I switched into Honors Chemistry after a week in the general ed one. The apathy and lethargy in the gen ed Chemistry class were strong from the beginning, and I didn't think I'd be pull off a repeat of Biology. It was a lot of work to keep your head down and blend in, and to be brave enough to pipe up with something witty when the time came. There would of course be class clowns who were at the top of their game. And as much as I would admire them from afar, I would still be in close enough proximity that there would be an expected response. I couldn't guarantee that I would know the right answer on time, when called on.

"This is Ben, he likes long walks on the beach," a student introduced his partner at the beginning of our ice-breaker activities. It was hilarious. These kids were going to be too funny again and I wouldn't be able to handle it.

I bumped into the gen ed chemistry teacher in the hallway a few weeks after my switch. She was young and very smiley. It was her first year teaching.

"I just wanted to let you know that you're doing a fine job," I said, "I just wanted more of a challenge."

"I understand completely," she said. "Sometimes we just need more of a challenge."

Or less of one.

On Limits

"So are you guys going to do the teen thing on the cruise?" Lauren asked us on the kids' side of the table. Us: me, her brother Erin, and my brother Mark. We were eating in a hotel restaurant in Alaska, the night before we would drive out to climb aboard the Coral Princess cruise ship.

"Probably not," Mark answered. Erin, Mark's age, and of similar personality laughed and added his thoughts about the program.

"I'll probably check it out the first night, just to see how lame it is, but I don't know if I'll go each time," Erin said.

As Lauren started her defense of "you guys, we might as well," I let my attention drift to my dad on the adult side of the table, who was recounting a David Sedaris essay to Lauren and Erin's parents—Joe and Leslie— and my mom. I was close enough to the adult side to listen to their conversation, although I was seated at the kid table, playing cards with them before our food arrived.

Mark and Erin by now had spent enough time together to enjoy making fun of each other.

"Hey Mark, how about those giant headphones?" Erin said, commenting on what Mark had brought along for his CD player.

"My name's Erin," Mark replied. "I like crème brûlée, and soufflés, and *parlez-vous francais*?" Mark's criticism of Erin was that he was high class. We had once been to his violin recital.

"You know what? I'm just not going to enjoy life as much, how about that?" he retorted.

Before the leaving for the cruise, I had asked my friend Bennett what I should expect on the cruise, as he had been on one.

"Oh man, cruises suck. It's like being in a hotel for a week, only there's no way to escape. Make sure to bring some books to read. Maybe brush up on your foreign languages because the workers are hired from all over the world. And, oh! You're 18 so you could probably go to the erotic comedy shows or whatever."

"Nah, dude, it's a family cruise," I said.

"Oh, well, okay. Oh, and never get drinks, they'll come around and offer you drinks, and you think they're free, but they're charging them to your bill the whole time. So only drink from the water fountains."

I shared Bennett's feelings about the cruise even before asking him. I had never wanted to go on the cruise. I wanted to stay home with my friends and the Columbia stuff I liked—going to concerts, maybe getting a job. Going on a cruise seemed like diving into classism—having others serving us at all time while we lay on recliners. There would need not be palm branches fanning us, as this was Alaska, but I imagined there would be some equivalent.

Boarding the cruise ship was a like a bizarro reverse Ellis Island experience. There were gates and queues to wait through, and suitcases to be pulled. It was metallic walls and echoes to begin with, before getting onto the ship with its luxury.

After we boarded and settled into our stateroom, Mark and I found the schedule of activities for the teenagers, listed in a binder titled *Off Limits: For Teens Only!* Somehow I noticed that it mentioned the age restrictions that defined teenager: 12-17 years old. I was 18, so I began to think I might be off the hook. I mentioned it to my dad, and he told me they would probably be fine with letting me join in the activities. We would have to wait and see, as the first meeting for Off Limits would be that evening.

After our first dinner, where I was apparently under-dressed, with jeans and my vintage flannel shirt not making the cut, I watched more of my *Manchurian Candidate* DVD. Then Mark and Erin knocked at the door.

"Scott are you ready to go to Off Limits? Hurry up, we don't want to be late to Off Limits!" Mark was giddy with anticipation of proving to everyone that he was so much radder than any other teenager who was going to Off Limits, typical teenage attitude. I immediately caught the spirit of jest and joined in.

"Okay let's do it, guys. Off Limits, here we come!" Erin, Lauren, Mark and I scampered through the halls of the ship towards the back, with the clique-ish confidence of sticking together, knowing we were cooler than anyone we would meet. Erin randomly jumped and touched the ceilings of the hallways as we scampered.

We arrived at the room, which was full of kids sitting in a circle of chairs, different than earlier that afternoon when my dad and I had gone to see about signing up, despite my age. The room was still colored brightly, with things placed appropriately diagonal everywhere to signify that this was a place for teenagers. Lil Jon played quietly on the room's jukebox. Mark and Erin took two open seats next to each other, leaving their siblings to fend for themselves. I sat across the room next to a boy with a lot of energy, glasses, a hat pulled down on his head, socks pulled high, Nike tennis shoes, shorts and a shirt with the name of some sports team.

"Oh man, I forgot gum!" he exclaimed.

"Here you go, man," I offered him a piece of Juicy Fruit I had in my pocket.

"All right, awesome! Thanks! I'll totally get you some next time I see you." Mark and Erin laughed at us from across the room. Then Erin asked me from across the room, "Hey, aren't you 18?" I laughed and shrugged it off, glad that no one was interested in further interrogation.

Then the team of adult supervisors got our attention. The leader was a young man named Craig, who said "eh" a lot.

"Okay, guys, the first thing we would like to do, as our icebreaker, is to play a game of human bingo. Did everyone get a paper?"

The kids in the circle nodded. The kid who I had given gum to nodded with a little extra energy.

"The object here is to go around the room and check off someone who represents each square. The first person to get the whole board filled wins a prize."

We set to work on bingo. Some kids putting effort into trying to be the first to finish, most kids putting effort into making sure everyone knew that they didn't care if they won or not. This was the trend for the other icebreaker games we would play. Our third icebreaker game was kind of like Simon Says, were the room was arranged into boy-girl pairs, where we were supposed to mimic the positions called out for us. My partner gave off a strong air of sarcasm towards the game, so I gave up too, and we just sat down while the rest carried on.

After the game was over, we were encouraged to sit around and talk unless we wanted to watch whatever movie won the popular vote. A girl named Ellen came and sat next to me, to talk to me about a band called Seether, which at first sounded interesting to me, but turned out to be something like Staind. I went ahead and took the liberty to scold everyone sitting near me for his or her music taste. On this cruise I had a chance to do so with authority, without my Columbia peers there to overshadow or mock me.

Erin noticed me chatting it up with our fellow Off Limiters, and decided to throw a wrench into our machine, possibly because he saw that I wasn't taking Off Limits in jest.

"Hey, are you 18 or something?" he asked while making eye contact with everyone near me. "Guys, I think he's probably 18."

"Ha, real funny, Erin," I said.

"Are you 18?" Ellen asked me.

"Well, I might be 18. It depends on what you mean by 18, really. Because, I mean, what is 18 after all?" I loved not giving a straight answer.

"Scott, if you're 18, why would you come to this teen thing then? Isn't it a little too young for you?" Ellen asked, launching me into my defense.

"What do you want me to do, Ellen? Aquacize? Pottery classes? I'm not an adult adult. Why not stick with my beloved family and newfound friends?"

By this point, Erin had moved off in the room to mention to some more kids that I was 18.

About fifteen minutes into whatever movie was playing, Craig came over and interrupted our conversation.

"Um, excuse me, Scott, are you 18?" he asked.

"Well... you could say that. Yes, I'm 18," I said, deciding now was a good time to give a straight answer.

"Okay, well, we've got rules here, and it's actually, only for ages 12 to 17," he explained to me. I couldn't believe that I was actually being arrested for being 18. "It's okay if you stay tonight, but I can't be responsible for you."

"Well, I came here earlier this afternoon and a lady told me it would be okay if I was here, just that you guys wouldn't be able to give me medicine in the case of an emergency."

"Well, actually, we're not going to be able to have you here," Craig said. Then Ellen jumped in.

"Oh, but we *like* Scott," she said.

"Well, yeah, I wish Scott could stay, too, but I've got these rules to follow." I could feel it. The training he must have gone through to get this job. Befriend the kids but stick to the regulations.

"It's all right, guys. I understand Craig. You've got rules to follow, and I'm not going to fight that. It's all right. I'm sure there will be other stuff for me to do on the cruise." I was milking it. Craig left after he was sure that I understood. We resumed the conversation, and then Erin came over again.

"Scott, did Craig tell you you couldn't come back?" Erin asked and laughed.

"Yeah, thanks a lot, Erin. Thanks for ruining my cruise. *This was all I had*."

"Dude, I'm so sorry, I totally didn't mean to get you kicked out. I thought you said they would let you stay."

"Yeah, that's what I thought but apparently... maybe if you hadn't been blabbing all that *aren't you 18* garbage then—"

"Oh God, I'm sorry. Man, you're totally never going to let this go are you?" Erin said.

"Yeah, we'll see."

I felt like a dirty old man, although I wasn't sure how I could feel so dirty and old for only being 18, not having done anything and only being on the cruise one night.

So far I had only spent time in the ship's library on a firm cushioned chair—like the kind at Grandma's house, reading a book I had brought myself – C.S. Lewis' *Mere Christianity*. A youth pastor had recommended it to me after a round of disc golf months before, and I was just now getting around to it. It was formative at that age—just like everything else I was taking in and exploring. Lewis wrote of politics, sexuality, and psychology and actually made arguments.

He compared sexual appetites and hunger. I read of his illustration that if you were in a country that gathered around to watch a strip-tease act of a piece of bacon on a covered plate, you'd think something was up. How much more then, to look at the sexual culture of the West and draw conclusions about the overwrought state of our sexual appetite.

Little did I know that I was further entering that world on the cruise. There were other people on the cruise, at that very moment, getting liquored up and having affairs. And for the young people, hormones were also raging and being kept in check.

Ellen decided that we should go play cards and so she went to pull Mark, Erin and Lauren from the movie while I waited outside. She came back outside the door while we waited for them to come out. There was a group of older girls also waiting outside, who had fled the evening as soon as the movie started, possibly sooner. Some of the girls were from Los Angeles. They wore short skirts, and poofy snow boots, which must have been on the verge of fashion in Los Angeles. They talked to Ellen while I waited off to the side.

"Gawd, this cruise sucks. Did you see any hot guys in there?"

"No, they're all totally lame. This guy has a good personality, though," Ellen said. I stepped farther away from them, trying to find a shadow. I assumed that I did not count as hot because I had shaven my own head earlier that summer, and the crew cut was only now growing out.

"I know, I'm so mad my parents made me go on this dumb Alaska cruise. I totally wanted to go on one on the Pacific, because the guys there are *so hot*," one of the girls said.

"Do you guys have any alcohol?" one of them asked. This went on for a while, then Mark, Erin and Lauren came out of Off Limits, and we walked off to go to the card room of the ship. But before that, we stopped in the cafeteria, which was always open and had pizza at all times. Ellen stopped to talk to some guys she had met earlier, so we lost her for a while.

Erin, Lauren, Mark and I sat at a table in the card room shuffling cards, not really playing.

"Scott, what are you going to do all week, now?" Mark asked.

"Yeah, man, I feel bad. How could I make it up to you?" Erin asked. I thought for a moment.

"What if we had like, another Off Limits thing, but it was like, the opposite of Off Limits?" I thought out loud. "Every night, after Off Limits gets over at midnight, we could have folks come from Off Limits to this card room, and then just chill. It will be like, anti-Off Limits. It will be On Limits."

They all laughed, not a disapproving laugh, though. They knew it was an awesome idea, but only Mark understood the implications of calling it On Limits.

"It will be like Master P, you know? No Limit? No Limit Soldiers? We will be On Limit Soldiers," I said. And then it was born. Mark and Erin pledged their allegiance and promised to recruit kids the following evening. Lauren rolled her eyes.

We played poker for a while, with improvised checkerboard pieces as poker chips. Later, Ellen walked into the room with her friend Victoria.

"There you are!" said Ellen, as they came and sat down with us. They were dressed up, as they had been at a dance, with the guys Ellen first got distracted by at the cafeteria. They said they had left the dance after the guys had lost their focus to girls that Ellen and Victoria referred to as "Barbies."

It was hard to place Ellen's background. She mentioned she had been adopted, but we did not know from what country. She was full figured, and if I had to guess a country I would have said Nepal. Victoria was tall and thin, with dark eyes and dirty blond hair. She gave her preferences on men as we sat.

"Long hair is way sexier on men," she said. Mark and I took this to heart. It would be a while until my crew cut grew out again.

They joined us in our game of poker, but soon the conversation became more important than the card game. We stayed up until 3 am, slaphappy.

"I feel like I've known you guys for years, and I've only been here for like, one night," Ellen said. We had become close enough that she dared a game of chicken on Mark and Erin, moving her hands up their thighs until one of them backed away. A few moments later, Victoria reached her socked foot into my thigh towards my groin, curious.

The next night, Erin and Mark had filled the card room with kids for On Limits. I showed up a little late to the meeting, but I still felt important because I was still wearing a tie from the night's dinner and the show I had gone to— horrible, horrible stand up comedy. I was pleased to see On Limits working out.

Erin played every song I requested of him on violin. A boy named Adam played some AC/ DC songs on an acoustic guitar. Mike, the brother of the girls from Los Angeles dominated everyone he played poker with. We had gotten to know him intimately at the cafeteria when he swallowed a handful of vitamins with his pizza. He mentioned that he had been known to take suppositories. I supposed it was an LA thing.

Much of my time on the cruise I spent solo wandering. I wandered through the upper levels of the solarium while listening to Nas' *Illmatic* on my portable CD player. I wandered out to the deck of the ship where Mom and Dad had spotted whales in the distance. There was a small office room which had two computers, with internet access for a fee. I wanted to send emails to my friends back home, but it wasn't worth it.

At dinner with Mom and Dad and Joe and Leslie, Dad practiced his Thai with the waiters. "*Čhạn mị phūd phās'ā thịy.*" He had learned to say "I don't speak _____" in many languages, including Thai. The waiter laughed when he heard it.

"You know what I appreciate about the people here?" Joe said. "Everyone is outgoing." He had a point. I just couldn't help but think that it was forced in someway. The hostess who seated us was from Romania. She mentioned that many of the people working on the cruise were from countries that had faced economic difficulties, so people were "motivated" to find work on the cruise. The maitre'd for the restaurant was Italian, but I think our Romanian hostess had adopted saying "*prego*" as well to go along with the Italian-themed restaurant.

One night, Mom and Dad encouraged me to find some time away from them. They were going to have an adults only dinner, unintentionally chipping away at the little socialization I actually had.

I made my way back to On Limits. It was the usuals of us around the card table. Then Ellen came in, dressed up, but sobbing.

"This is why I hate being adopted," she said. Victoria tried to console her, finding out what had happened. Apparently, there had been drama in her cabin. Her parents had threatened to kick her out, even putting her suitcase outside the door. It hurt to think that something so tragic could happen to one of us, whom we had come to love, on a cruise, with all of its glamorous appearances. At the same time, it was encouraging that she had come to us. We had built something.

In my wandering, I had discovered the jazz lounge. It had a chill vibe, with deep leather chairs. The perfect place for eavesdropping and writing. I carried my Palm Pilot with me and jotted notes when I could. I invited Ellen to meet me at the jazz lounge. She took her time getting there.

A quartet played softly "Unforgettable" while an elderly couple danced. The singer talked them into one more song, a slow one. After the dance, I heard the singer talking to his band. There had been a flu outbreak a few months before on the ship, and the singer was recounting the struggle.

"I met with the manager in his office, and I told him, do you know what kind of credit card this is? You have to make a certain amount of money to get this maximum limit."

He was explaining why he didn't feel he should be subject to the quarantine, with the terms such as they were. He continued, "And I told him, rice is not a staple of a diet. You cannot survive on rice." I was enthralled to hear stories confirming the juicy underbelly of life on the ship that I suspected.

Ellen arrived.

"Isn't it marvelous, the jazz?" I said.

"Whatever," she laughed. She was dressed up, again. We moved out into the hallway, either because she was not allowed in, or because I wanted to share music of my own with her. I had burned her a CD. A band from my hometown, The Pows, had come up with some garage rock. I played the first song for her, which sounded like "Stray Cat Strut."

"I like the beat," she said, the same response the kids always used on *American Bandstand*.

"How about this one?" I said, reaching into my leather case of CD's. "My boy Nas."

"Nas? You mean the guy who did that kids' song, 'I Know I Can'"?

"Oh come on, that's not his best. You've got to hear *God's Son*. He's a storyteller." I held up the earbuds for Ellen.

We were bonding. I couldn't believe it. It was like having a fresh start, on the cruise. We were both thrown into it, looking for connection and a place to belong. And we found it, quickly and easily. That was the miracle of it.

When I returned to Missouri, I spent a day and a night at the Summer Welcome getting ready to attend the university in the fall. Much like *Off Limits*, the day was filled with ice breaker activities, presentations, and the hopeful pairing off with buddies. I was fortunate to meet Evan. He was into EDM and DDR. I judged him for his music taste. He also thought I was weird for my Christian sexual ethic, but we were together.

That evening sleeping in the dorms for the first time, I wandered alone past the lounge and noticed some guys hanging out inside.

"Anything cool happening in here?" I asked.

"Nope. Fresh out," they snarked back. They would not be my friends. But others would be. We would make a way.

Sandwich Shop

It was February. There were four regular articles of clothing I wore to work at the sandwich shop to allow them to get disgusting and smelling of grilled meat. My oversized New Balances, which had become tainted with some eternal gummy residue from the sandwich shop's tiled floor. My khaki pants, which were required as opposed to jeans. The yellow oversized store t-shirt I wore daily, even with ketchup stains. And my grandpa's tight fitting suede jacket—which warmed me from the short walk where I parked my car into the mall.

This morning my coworker, technically a shift manager, Brian met me at my car. We walked in together.

"So, yesterday, Roger discovered a bag of marijuana in the back," he said stopping me just short of the employee entrance. "And the answer is, we don't know anything about it."

Roger was the franchise owner. He owned our sandwich shop, as well as one or two in St. Louis. When he came into town, he almost never smiled, like an anti-Santa Claus, and we were all naughty.

"How did it get there?" I asked Brian.

"A few weeks ago we were having a good time with the compression tanks. We realized if we unhooked the soda dispensers in the back, we could stuff stuff into the tubing and then shoot it out. Someone had a bag of weed and so

49

we stuffed it in and shot it out, but couldn't find it. Roger found it. So if he asks about it, the answer is we don't know how it got there," Brian shrugged.

"Man. This isn't fair," I said. "He's going to think it was me because I'm the goofiest one."

We entered and found Roger there ahead of us in the back office. This was the same office where Brian often sketched crude drawings of Roger and other employees in Microsoft Paint. A notable drawing involved Roger as Mr. Krabs, the restaurant owning character from *SpongeBob Squarepants*.

This was my first job out of college.

After graduation, I'd searched for jobs into the summer. One day in July of that year, I ended up at the mall food court. On a whim, I found myself standing at the counter to the sandwich shop talking to Brian at the cash register. I first met him in 8th grade P.E. class, where he wore the És brand skateboard shoes. This should have been a bonding element for us, as I was getting into skating, but I was silent almost always, crippled by shyness. This led to resentment amongst the other talkative students like Brian. Was I too good to talk?

"We should all be more like Scott," he had snarked when the P.E. teacher complimented me on something. "Scott, Scott, Scott, what an upstanding, responsible student. We should all be more like him."

However, as I began to speak more at the end of high school and entered Brian's friend group, he warmed to me. By the time we hit college, our games of midnight baseball at the American Legion field solidified our positive association with each other. Whenever I saw him and the gang working at the sandwich shop at the mall, I'd stop by for a hi and some laughs.

"You're looking for work?" Brian asked me at the counter.

"Yep," I said.

"You could apply here," he said.

"Really? What do I have to do?"

"Write your availability down here," he said, sliding me a brown paper napkin.

I had plenty of free time. I wrote 9 to 6 for most of the weekdays, except for Thursdays when I needed to be at Granny's House to volunteer at 4:30. For Sunday, I just wrote "Jesus."

This was the napkin David the manager picked up when I went in for my interview. I had worn green slacks that we had retrieved from my Grandpa's closet after he died. They were a little short, high-waters, and I wore them with brown dress shoes that had grown a little snug. I looked like Bart Simpson going to church.

"So are you a religious guy?" David asked me, concerned.

"Not really, I'm just really busy on Sundays and wouldn't be able to work," I said to dodge the discomfort of the question. Some would distinguish following Jesus from religion. There's trying to be good, then there's Jesus, the only one who was truly good, saving his followers. I didn't feel capable of getting into such nuances upon first meeting my boss.

It turned out he took off Sundays as well. The other coworkers would joke that it was a Catholic holdover. His other day off was Wednesday, to follow up after pool night.

I started the next day. David and I opened the store at 9am. The third employee would not arrive until 11am, when more of the lunch rush began. One of my duties consisted of slicing up green peppers. Initially I cut the peppers by carving out around the stem, and slicing away the white portion on the inside ridges. David caught me doing this and showed me a faster way—slicing the pepper completely in half, through the top, the stem, and then carving away the top and leaving the white portions inside.

"It'll cook away," he said. "And look at this, Catholic and Protestant getting along, getting work done."

Tim was the first to show up, walking around the corner as I peeked over the flat grill and through our glass that walled it off.

"Hey Belden."

"Hey Tim." I knew him from the skatepark. He was slightly shorter than me, and donned a goatee on occasion to mock David's standard facial hair.

"What are you up to?" he said.

"Oh, just doing a little *pepp* work," I said, triumphant in my pun. I would not know that my joke had landed home until the next day, when I stood near the cash register with him and Brian. Apparently the gossip about me traveled while I was away.

"*Pepp* work, huh?" Brian said as he leaned his cup against the soda dispensing machine to fill it with Pepsi. I did not realize it would automatically shut off when filled.

"Oh that's interesting, you're a lean-to man," I commented. "I'm more of a control guy. I prefer to hold the cup the whole time." Tim and Brian started laughing, not realizing what a nerd they had hired.

"Belden, that is some ferocious arm hair," Brian said.

"Thank you, should I comb it?" Somehow the topic of wrists came up, and Brian rose to defend his own.

"What are you talking about? I've got that beef wrist. *Uhn!*" he said, grunting. I was suddenly insecure about the size of my wrist.

My station would end up being cashier. They were under the impression that I was the nicest employee there, which wasn't saying much. Somehow, all of the employees were male. We were probably breaking the law at some level, but I was thankful to have a job, and it was hard to imagine how a female employee might fit in with all of us.

By the time I worked there, there was already an established tradition of homoerotic horseplay.

"Oh, I'll touch another man's crotch, no problem," Greg said, standing with me up front. "Come here, Tim." Tim sat on the counter next to the nacho cheese dispenser on the counter behind us. He lifted up his apron and Greg nonchalantly patted his crotch. Incredible. This was par for the course. Grabbing of the crotch was almost a sort of greeting, something like dogs sniffing each other's behinds. Eric, another employee, told me of a time before I had worked there when "the raptor claw" was the thing to look out for.

"Basically, what it was was, you'd be working on grill, and a man would come up from behind you and just *reeeaah!*" he said, imitating a raptor call while gesturing a hooked raptor's claw with his fingers.

I learned quickly that pranks were an essential part of working there. I kept my soda on a shelf below the cash register, in front of all of the other styrofoam cups locked away in plastic sheaths. We were forbidden to have our drinks above counter level, a regulation I recalled from working at Subway years before. As I reached for my sip of diluted root beer, I was disgusted to find a taste in my mouth that I couldn't place. I looked back toward the grill to see Brian and Tim laughing. Malt vinegar. Few people even put it on their fries.

"Just imagine being all sweaty on grill, reaching down for a gulp of Mountain Dew, and winding up with a mouthful of ketchup," Brian said. It seemed like all of the truly epic debauchery had gone on before I had started working there. And yet the tradition was still carrying on strong.

It was called "Jamesing" money from the cash register, named for a former employee who never had trouble buying Dairy Queen or Orange Julius a few stores down.

"That's a *felony*," my accounting friend informed me, as I sat next to him in Barnes & Noble recounting the antics of the day.

The cash register itself had some buttons that were probably against the law. Buttons were programmable on this beige plastic that reminded me of an Apple L2. Orders would show up on the monitor stationed above the grill, in green text on the black background. But so would customized comments like "would," which was short for "would have sexual relations with said customer." It made sense of what I had heard one of the guys say under his breath when standing with me up front and watching girls walk by. I thought they had been saying "wood," but it turned out to be the homophone "would" which was perhaps slightly less crass. On the cash register was also the $0.15 Dumb Tax button, which was definitely against the law. That one was riskier, because it would show up on the customer's receipt. But there were times when it felt like you really needed to let the customer have it. One such time was Steak-Sub girl.

"I'll have the steak sub," said the girl with long fake eyelashes standing before me.

"Which one? There are many."

"The one right there. 'Steak sub.'"

"Oh, you mean the Philly cheesesteak?"

"No. I'm reading it right there, *steak sub*."

I turned around to look at our menu again.

"Oh. I'm sorry. That's the category."

"Ok fine," she said. "I'll take the cheesesteak then." It was tense as I worked up her order on the cash register.

"You new?"

"I'm sorry?"

"Are you new here?" she asked.

"No, I've been working here for a while." I handed her her receipt and she continued around the corner to wait for her sandwich—her steak sub. I received some relief from the customers behind her in line. A humorous exhale, a smile, anything small to let me know that they had seen what I had been through.

The most difficult part of the job did not come from customers. Randy, an employee we hired about four months after me would rock my 22 year-old world. He was a friend of the other employees— that's how most of us got hired. We were all goofy. Much of what the guys did was immature. And sure, I regressed in maturity a few years just working there—at a job I could have potentially had in high school. The raptor claw, touching another man's crotch. It was goofy and silly, yet there was some levity to it. With Randy, it seemed like there wasn't.

He played too rough. And he didn't know when to stop. Even when I tried to confront him about it at work, he would seem to just bulldoze by, and not hear me. There was an afternoon where we switched roles. He took the cash register and I tried grill for a while. It was only the two of us. I was already slow on grill. I just didn't possess the multitasking ability to work on multiple sandwiches at the same time and keep things going. But Randy, as well as being gruff or brusque with customers, appeared to have no concern for my predicament on grill.

"Randy, could you slow down a bit?"

"What's wrong, Belden?"

"It's just like, I can't keep up. I don't think I'm cut out for this."

"Oh wow! You are behind, Belden."

"I know. I'm not used to grill. I think we need to switch back. I'm just burning these sandwiches and it's not working out."

"Okay, let's switch then." He barged back to the grill, almost bumping into me. Courtesy was absent. It felt like a land devoid of mercy, where those bigger and faster ruled like dinosaurs and I didn't stand a chance.

The very presence of someone who seemed so insensitive felt crushing and oppressive, whether he was at work or not. Hat Girl—a friendly girl who worked at Lids down the hallway—saw my near tears as I returned to the cash register.

"Are you doing okay?" she said. In Hat Girl, mercy had arrived for a moment, but she would not be able to rescue me.

"I'm doing okay. We are just a little busy today," I said, strained.

I happened to mention the conflict with Randy to my pastor after a morning Bible study.

"I just don't think I can do it anymore," I said. "I don't think it'd be good for me to quit my job just because of this but I feel like if it builds up I might kill him."

"Do you wish you could just grab his face and smash it down into the grill?"

"Yeah, actually, that'd do it, I think," surprised at how well the pastor had read the situation. It was like in *Analyze This* when Robert DeNiro feels good after shooting a pillow.

Simply saying it out loud to the pastor helped me to know what needed to be done. With all the negative feelings churning in me, I realized I needed to confront Randy. He didn't seem to listen to me at work. So I would call him when we were off the clock.

At night, I sat in my car in my parents' driveway in the dark in the cold.

"Hi Randy, we need to talk," I said.

"Okay, sure."

"Is now a good time?" I asked.

"I'm dropping my brother off. Can I give you a call back in a few minutes?"

"Sure."

I waited. My car was a keg of dynamite, but I thought over what I wanted to say. It was going to be a controlled explosion, with the goal of blasting away enmity so that we could get back to work.

A few minutes later the phone rang. I answered.

"Things aren't working out," I said.

"Oh," he replied.

"You might not realize it, but you're hurting me at work. If you bump into me, or whatever else you do. I need you to stop."

"Okay. I'm sorry. I didn't realize it. I thought we were just playing around."

"Yeah, well we weren't. I need you to stop that crap."

"Okay, sorry."

I hung up. I breathed heavily and it was difficult to sleep that night. Would what I had said to him take?

The next day at work, it was like people had spaced out from me. I didn't know what the consequences would be, but I did not expect it to be the other guys feeling like they couldn't joke with me.

"Belden said we can't touch him anymore," Jon-tan said.

"It wasn't so much all of y'all, just Randy," I said. But it didn't hurt to have it all stop. If as a Christian I was supposed to be salt and light, having a redeeming influence on those around me, I was very surprised at the circumstances that hat brought about change. Perhaps I was Hamlet, waiting too long while everything around me crumbled. Nevertheless, I was happy to now have room to breathe.

A young friend of ours from the skatepark would just come by to hang out. We let him into the back room and he sat for much of the day on top of a stack of boxes. I had brought in a burned CD from high school. It had a song from 2 Live Crew that I had heard on *The Chris Rock Show* —"Can a n____ get a table dance?" We played it on loop on the old stereo in the back.

"I've been listening to this for the past half-hour," Tyler said.

"Look man, you could be doing things," I said. "You could learn guitar or something like that." Instead he was just waiting for his girlfriend to get off of work.

At the same time, I thought of my coworkers and I. How long would we be working at the sandwich shop?

There was a day where I stood with Tim up front. Out in the food court there was a table of HVAC employees sitting together eating sandwiches.

"Is that going to be us?" Tim asked. "All hanging out together, just a few years older, with slightly more facial hair, checking out the slightly younger girls that are walking by? And Brian will still be five years old."

In February, I received an interview to do substitute teaching. I showed up to the interview having not turned in one of the question sheets.

"Go ahead and complete this and then you can come on in to talk," the woman interviewing me said, handing me the paper while I sat in the chair in the waiting room.

I was a little unnerved to be put on the spot like this. I was used to typing up answers on my computer and then looking back over them. Here I would be writing in pen, and would have to go straight off the top of the dome. I muddled through it and then knocked on the woman's door.

During the interview, we spent most of the time talking about my study abroad experience in Senegal. It seemed that she had already made up her mind to hire me before we started. I was blown away at almost how easy it was.

"There will be some hard days," she said. "Kids can be a lot. There will be days where you go home and you're just exhausted. But there are also days where you'll go home knowing that you had a really good day, and that you made a difference."

The next day, I wrote David my two-weeks' notice on a piece of paper.

"Can you hear them, David? They're blowing. The winds. *Whheewww wheeww*. Winds of change. I've had a good time here. But now, in the words of Lynyrd Skynyrd, "I'm as free as a bird now. And this bird you cannot change."

Brian took my notice and posted it up on the bulletin board in the back. The same place Roger had posted the bag of marijuana. It had a note next to it. "I'm guessing I need to contact the Columbia Police Department about this?"

"I have no idea how it happened," I had heard Brian say to Roger through the swinging door behind me.

Brian soon joined me at the front of the store next to the cash register.

"By the way, you had the Skynyrd lyrics wrong," he told me. "It's 'this bird you cannot chain' not 'change.'"

"Oh, point noted."

As we looked out into the café court we saw the giant carousel at the center of it all. It constantly filled the corridor with circus music, so much so that after a while you stopped noticing it. Round and round it went, until someone finally put an end to the zaniness and it was time to get off.

The Coolest Man I Ever Met

"Did I miss the dress code, guys? What's up with all the button-downs?" He was spot on. I admit that I had fallen in line. In Sociology of Psychology class, I had learned about the experiments where the planted group members all agreed that a round line was straight, until the newbie test subject in the experiment finally gave in against his will. Resistance is futile. So after my first summer of linguistics grad school in North Dakota where I wore t-shirts, I quickly joined the rest with collared short-sleeve button downs. There were homeschoolers among us. And I was self-conscious about neck hair.

Sean, however, was freshly arrived. Very fresh. He had heard about the summer linguistics program on a whim from one of his professors, and made the trip from Shanghai to Grand Forks to join us. It was my third summer, his first. We were stationed in the same dorms, on the same floor, with him just a few doors down on the other side. My roommate this year, Ben, was a stalwart of button-down collared shirts, and also home schooled. He listened to worship music in French on his computer. I appreciated the introduction to it, having something to fill our room's silence, noting that Ben probably wouldn't be interested in the Wu Tang Clan on my own computer.

Ben and I made our way down the hallway to Sam's room to walk together to the first day's registration meeting. And Sean was roommates with Sam.

Sean was tall, with long hair, as we imagined Jesus would be. He was very smiley, ENFP, almost surfery, until I asked why he went by Sean, rather than his name written on the door. His face went flat and he fell silent. I had touched on something I didn't completely understand. In that moment, I already feared that I risked losing him.

The welcome address for our program was the same I had heard for the past two summers. The director explained that the exhilaration of the eight-week session was part of the rush. He warned us of the potential reasons students might fall behind—either by spending too much time on particular assignments, or by staying up and socializing— or, ironically, by doing both.

Then, he mentioned what we all needed to hear each summer.

"Some of you come here expecting a Christian school experience. That is, many come here for training in linguistics to be able to serve overseas as a missionary, especially in Bible translation. So you might expect the student body makeup to be similar to that of a Christian college. Others of you come expecting a secular school experience, as this is the University of North Dakota. You might expect the demographics to be similar to those of a traditional public school. The reality is that neither assumption is correct."

I looked across the auditorium to see Sean sitting next to Sam. I wondered if they realized just how different they would be. Somehow I knew early on that Sam had attended a fundamentalist Christian university. The little I knew about the school was that there was a haircut rule. The males were not to have their hair touching their ears or collars. I had a very negative experience with haircut rules. It was part of what kept my brothers and me form attending a Christian sports camp in southern Missouri. Charitably put, perhaps they were concerned that students with long hair would get it caught in the zip-line or something like that. However, in later years I learned that it was something about taking an "all American pledge."

"Those are the kind of upstanding, open and receptive people I'd like to be with," my older brother said sarcastically, pony-tailed since ninth grade.

I waited to see what it would be like for Sean and Sam to get to know each other.

The second night in, I heard Sean down the hallway talking to another returning student, James. I only caught bits and pieces of their conversation, though I tried to catch the whole thing.

"Yeah, I've been living in Shanghai for the past…. years… skateboarding…"

James was undoubtedly hooked. It was just a get-to-know-you chat, but Sean was cooler and cooler with each scrambled and deciphered word. Many of us in the program had been overseas or had relatives overseas, but none of us were professional skateboarders. The black sheep had arrived, and he was awesome.

Wilkerson Dining Hall was where we linguistics students did all of our socializing between classes. The program had worked out a deal where we didn't have to pay as much for the traditional dining plan, because apparently we didn't waste as much food as the traditional students. I like to think that it was the home-school upbringing in half of us— raised right.

I worked up the nerve to sit next to Sean at dinner.

"How about a trip to the skatepark?" I said.

"Let's do it. When are you thinking?"

"How about after dinner here?"

"Sounds good."

We drove to the skatepark. He caught me up on his time in Shanghai. He had worked different jobs while having a lot of free time to skate. He showed me pictures from his time as a preschool teacher. He was standing up and marching around as the students seated in a circle got up to follow him. A positive attitude and a heart for kids— what more could you want? People were following him as soon as they could.

When we got out to skate at the skatepark, a few other local skaters were there. I had not talked much to any of them, except for one guy, Brian. Two summers before, I had stopped skating just long enough to ask if there were any other good skateparks in nearby towns, besides Fargo.

"If you've got a passport, I'd head up to Winnipeg," Brian told me. There was an entire skate plaza that had been built in the recent years. I made the trip up after my second summer.

This day, with Sean, all attention was on Sean. He skated obstacles with speed and fearlessness that I had only slowly stumbled around on. He grabbed the admiration of everyone watching as he went up for a wallie to blunt slide on the concrete Jersey barrier.

"It doesn't even make sense," one of the other skaters near me said. I had not been this proud of bringing along an acquaintance since midnight baseball in college, when I brought a friend who was able to swing for the fences. They called him Wonderboy.

It might not be accurate to say that I was riding Sean's coattails. I still said little to all the other skaters. Instead, I was standing by, basking in glory by association. He had ridden in my car. I had something to offer.

We made our way back to the car after skating.

"This summer is going to be just fine," Sean said. "I've got a friend to skate with."

In the ride back to the car, he broached the question that had not been discussed yet.

"So, are you interested in Bible translation?" he asked. I took a moment. I did not want to deny Jesus, but I did not want him to think I was cut of the same button-down cloth as his roommate with the university's haircut rule.

"Ah, I have to say," I said, weighing my words, "I'm thankful for Bible translators, but I don't think it's for me." He looked somewhat relieved, but also wary. Why was I there, then? I continued.

"I'm interested in being a literacy specialist. I want to go back to Senegal," I said.

"Senegal, huh?"

"Yeah, it was great. I'm hoping to go back. That's the whole plan for this literacy training."

"All the Senegalese guys I knew in Shanghai were coke dealers."

"Impressive."

"I'm not saying they're all bad guys, but it was just everyone I knew in Shanghai, they sold coke."

I made a joke about cocaine. Sean responded with, "I think a blunt will do it for me." He was also testing the waters, finding out how much of each other we'd be comfortable with. Was I his roommate? Or was I someone who could have been his roommate in Shanghai— where the courtyard was full of marijuana plants because the police didn't know what they were looking for?

By the second Friday, Sean had already made friends with guys from the skatepark and he knew where the parties were in town. He had biked to the skatepark with his board on his own time during the week.

We sat with him around a table of pitchers of beer and pizza on the rooftop of Rhombus Guys pizzeria. It was an ideal spot for bonding. There were Christmas lights strung about that made everything glow with romance and potential. The summer before they had played *The Big Lebowski* on the big screen, while the mosquito killing lights ran strong all around us.

Sean had corralled the group of us—Andrea, Rachel and Sarah, with Ryan as well. I ordered a Red Stripe and took my time with it.

"Scott, are you one and done?" Andrea asked. I didn't know what she meant.

"I mean you just drink one beer and that's it?" she explained.

"Oh, then, yeah, I guess so. I have low tolerance," I said. "Plus, I'm driving." I told the story of having been pulled over after drinking a non-alcoholic O'Doul's.

"The police officer asked me, 'Son, have you had anything to drink?' I said, 'Funny enough, an O'Doul's!'"

Sean sat approximately at the center of the long table, like Jesus in Da Vinci's Last Supper. Except instead of a disciple leaning back on him, at one point in the evening, one of the girls leaned across Sean's lap with her arms, flirtatiously, asking for a piece of pizza. *That is some non-verbal communication!* I thought. *You can do this?* It turned out girls were fawning over him, too. His charisma broke the gender barrier.

Brian from the skatepark showed up a little later with his skateboard.

"A real skate rat" Sean had remarked to me. "Someone always down to skate." Brian told us that there was a bonfire happening at Mikey's house. I got in my car with Ryan and headed in that direction. It was not far from downtown, so Brian biked there.

Ryan, from the East Coast, had worked as a plumber before deciding to switch into missionary work. He and his wife were anthropologists, and they were anticipating going to the field. There were not that many anthropologists in the missions organization they were joining. Not really knowing what to do with them, the leadership sent them to our linguistics camp for a summer. They had two children with them that summer at the program and in his spare time Ryan was reading a book called *The Sex Lives of Cannibals*. Though his wife and kids were back at the dorms, Ryan seemed to be in his element hanging out with twenty-somethings looking for a party.

We arrived in the quiet neighborhood not far from downtown. The whole area was very flat, and each of the small houses fit the grid work of these quaint neighborhoods. There were sparse trees. We parked our cars in a nearby driveway and Sean lead the way to the campfire. A group of people in punk and skate clothing sat around the fire. Cans of PBR abounded. Sean introduced us to the group. There was a large man who was a little drunk, speaking with an Irish accent.

"I'm Irish," he said.

"That's great," I said. "You mean you're from Ireland or you have Irish heritage?"

"I'm Irish," he said.

"Me too. My grandpa's dad came straight over on a boat." I was just trying to keep up. This man was much larger than me. I would not have started a conversation with him in the streets if he had been sober.

"How old are you?" he asked me, the way Fat Bastard in *Austin Powers* might have interrogated Mini-Me.

"Twenty five," I said. I wonder what made him think I was younger. Perhaps it was the glasses I was wearing that implied fragility. But more likely, the collared polo.

Rachel and Andrea needed to use the bathroom. Sean found Mikey, who led us into the house. It felt wild outside, but there was some reprieve being inside. I scoped out the artwork on the fridge while waiting for the girls. When we returned outside, Mikey had climbed onto the top of the roof with his skateboard.

"Who's ready to see me land this?" he asked. The crowd of people around the fire moved in the direction of where he'd be jumping off the house. He was crouched, and planned to land on his skateboard in the grass of his yard. He landed with a loud crash just past the bushes. This brought over his neighbor, a large motherly figure.

"I swear to God, Mikey, we've been over this before. No more jumping off the roof, or I'll call the cops."

"I'm sorry," he said, slurred.

"No, sorry doesn't cut it," she said. "You just need to cut this crap out. Or I'll call the police and they can just send all of you home."

We decided it was time to go. Sean knew of yet another party going on that night.

As I ducked into my driver's seat, the large Irish man came and urged a beer in my face.

"Drink this," he said, standing over me.

"No thanks, I'm about to drive," I said.

"Just drink it," he said.

"I don't think it'd be a good idea." He wasn't going to take no for an answer. Sean reached over from the back seat and took the can out of his hand, intercepting the pressure, drinking it down. A mediator.

We arrived at the parking lot for the Canada Inn. There was a waterpark attached to the hotel, though I had never been here during the previous two summers in Grand Forks. The previous summer, our language nurturer for Kirundi had a part-time job making pizzas at the hotel.

One of the girls hopped onto Sean's back as he carried her piggyback style into the hotel. Brian led us into the hotel to the room where one of the skateboarders' girlfriend was having a birthday party. The room was full of people as we entered.

The birthday girl welcomed us and gave a big hug to Sarah.

"Aww, you're so cute and smiley," she said, causing Sarah to smile even more. The birthday girl was a little drunk, holding a cup in her hand while her tube top held the rest of her up. Her boyfriend was tall and stood nearby, a classy version of the "Irish" man I had met at the bonfire.

I didn't really feel like mingling in this crowd where people were already talking to each other. Nor did the other girls, really. Sean comforted us by making conversation with us in the corner of the room. He talked about school.

"I'm realizing that a lot of the skate community I lived with in Shanghai would make for a great study in sociolinguistics," Sean said. I was along for the ride, whatever he wanted to say next.

"For example," he continued, "we really had our own community of practice going on. Even in the terminology we'd use for skate tricks. You could probably tell a lot from different skaters just based on what term they used for '360 flip.'"

How had Sean already made learning seem so cool, and tied it into real life within a week of being there? It was all validation for us. It was okay to be a skateboarder. A linguist. A nerd. A nerd at a party not easily integrating. It was warmth lifting us up as we were.

For the rest of the summer, Sean would get closer to Ryan. They were taking the Package A set of courses as first year students: Syntax & Morphology, Second Language Acquisition, Articulatory Phonetics, and Sociolinguistics. As returning students, my roommate Ben and I were in Package B courses: Phonology, Field Methods, and Anthropology. Sean would eat dinner with Ryan's family at an earlier hour, then I'd show up closer to 6:30 when the cafeteria was about to close.

I once watched Sean moving in the direction of the cafeteria with Ryan's family. He was cruising on his skateboard with them at a leisurely pace, and attempted a trick called a big spin. Effortlessly, and with style. Ryan's kids jumped up and down as he did it. It was the way things were supposed to be. Little ones drawn to displays of power and love.

Sean went on a weekend trip with two other younger first year students to Winnipeg, where they stopped by the giant skatepark Brian had told me about. One of the students had footage of Sean shredding the bowl. He had seemingly captured him, and yet he wasn't mine.

Then one afternoon, Rachel came up to me in the basement booths where we studied.

"So, my language helper for Field Methods is trying to set me up with a friend," she said. Rachel was in a group learning a language from Cameroon.

"That sounds pretty good," I said. "Free boyfriend."

"Well, we'll see. There's a party, but I don't think I want to go alone."

"Ah, what kind of party?"

"An African dance party."

"Oh?" I said. I had not danced since my study abroad trip in Senegal, when I learned the appeal of night clubs. Places of sin, yet fun.

Here was a friend in need. Rachel spread the word to Andrea and Sean.

The night of the party, I was in my dorm room spraying myself with cologne. I was also wearing an oversized plaid button-down shirt, since it felt like dressing up. I didn't tuck it in.

"Why are you getting all spruced up?" another classmate asked me.

"African dance party, no big deal" I said.

"You looking for a lady?" Sean, standing nearby, raised an eyebrow.

"Nah, I just want to smell good," I lied.

Sean, Andrea, Rachel and I headed outside where Rachel's suitor was waiting in a silver sedan with tinted windows. We watched from a distance at the door to the building while she talked to him from outside the car.

"No thanks, I think I'll ride with my friends," she told him. "See you there."

We hopped into my car and heard to the Episcopal Church downtown. The dance party would be in the church's basement. When we arrived in the parking lot someone came up to me in the dark.

"Scott?" he said. It was Pranith, our language helper for Field Methods. We were studying Marathi with him.

"Pranith!" I said. "Good to see you. Are you here for the party?"

"Yes," he said. "My roommate told me about it."

"Excellent." Pranith was tall and calm. He was in Grand Forks to study engineering. And I knew he liked going to parties. That was always his question to us, his students— "What do you do on the weekends?" Now he would find out.

We walked inside and discovered a meal had been prepared for us all. We found a seat at the long tables around the perimeter of the basement. There were probably thirty others in the basement, Africans from different countries. One of the students offered up a prayer to begin everything. Then we went up to serve ourselves at the buffet. I had a feeling one of the pots was pieces of stomach and intestines, but Rachel and Andrea said they didn't want to know what they were eating. I picked up a malt beverage. There was no alcohol at this event.

After eating the same student who had offered up the prayer gave us all an exhortation to begin dancing, repeating the phrase "put on your dancing shoes." And it was on.

We watched from our table at first, and then were beckoned to the dance floor, especially by Rachel's suitor. It was African music, mixed in with hip-hop. Wiz Khalifa's "Black and Yellow" played.

I broke off to speak French and dance with a nursing student during a slower song. Someone else came up to join her but she shooed him away, saying "*Je veux danser avec le blanc*"— 'I want to dance with the white guy.'

When a Congolese song came on, the inevitable circle was formed. We each took turns going into the center and doing a move. I was nudged forward, and not knowing what else to do, did a dramatic stomp in the middle. The circle erupted and I found my spot back in the circle next to Sean.

The music mix slowed down for a while as more people arrived. I took a moment to stand off to the side and talk to Pranith. In addition to working on his Master's Degree and helping us with Marathi, he worked in the kitchen at Wilkerson Dining Hall.

"Hey, isn't that that girl from the dining hall?" I asked him, recognizing one of his coworkers.

"Yeah, go say hi."

"Nah, not right now." A few minutes later I looked and she was talking to a tall, attractive man in a baseball cap.

"That's what happens when you hesitate," Pranith said.

The music mix moved to salsa. A petite woman in white dress sweated as she danced with a man across from her. We bade farewell to those that had invited us. Rachel's suitor asked her to marry him, but she cordially turned him down.

We climbed into my car with Pranith and made our way to his apartment. It was nearing one AM. His roommate was not home. Pranith offered us beer, and we moved into the living room where he got the hookah going. Sean and Andrea sat on the couch. Rachel and I sat on the floor.

The conversation flowed freely. Pranith asked us about our experience studying linguistics there for the summer, including what it was like to be in a community with religious practitioners.

Sean opened it up.

"It's not easy," he said. "People assume a lot of things about you, and they don't know the whole story."

Sean continued.

"I was in my room. And a friend of my roommate stopped by. Normally I like to talk to people, but in this case, he was basically cornering me, asking me why I wasn't a Christian. He asked me if I had read any C.S. Lewis. It kept going, until it got to the point where I essentially had to say, 'Look, we're going to stop talking now.'"

It was a revelation for us. Jesus called his disciples to fish for people, but not corner them. We did not like to think of our friend as trapped against his will, especially if it was by someone allegedly representing our "team."

"I'm sorry you had to experience that," I said. I sensed in Rachel, sitting near me on the floor, the strange mixture of concern and empathy.

Sean invited each of us to share our own stories. We took turns doing so. Rachel told the story of the denomination she grew up in, and how there was a split in recent years. Andrea told the story of preparing for seminary, and some of the books she was reading. I told the

74

story of one of my previous roommates, where our differences in background made things tough for a time, but upon open hearted confession and discussion we grew to love each other. It had happened before, and thankfully, it was happening again.

Towards the end of the evening, Pranith asked us, "Do you guys want to see a picture of my god?"

"Sure," we said. It was a shared vulnerability for all of us.

Pranith went into his room and brought out a picture of his goddess. It was a brightly colored drawing, reminiscent of what I had seen in drawings of the *Bhagavad-Gita.* Pranith told us the tale of how his goddess had received a sword to attack her enemy on behalf of her people. It struck me that Pranith might not have felt comfortable sharing this with me during our language elicitation sessions. But after a night of partying, dancing, and hookah, we had built up enough trust with each other that openness was flowing.

In Pranith's living room, we eventually heard chirping outside. We looked up to the window and saw that dawn was coming. We had partied and hung out until 5am.

We would not be going to church that Sunday. We hopped in the car and made the short drive back to the dorms.

"How about that?" Sean said in the car. "It's not everyday that you get to see somebody's god."

Sean and I made our way back to the men's wing of the dorms while the ladies went to theirs. We retrieved our toothbrushes from our rooms in silence, trying not to wake up our roommates who would be church-bound in a few hours.

We went to the dorm bathrooms at the end of the hall. The windows were open as there was no air conditioning in these North Dakota dorms. Outside were the tall trees with branches swaying above the coulee. We brushed our teeth. With mouths full of toothpaste, we complimented each other.

"That stomp," Sean said, pointing to me. "At first I was like, *what is he doing? He just stopped.* Then everyone went crazy and I was like, *oooooh, that was epic.*"

"Ha," I said. "Thanks man." He continued gushing.

"How did you know that that was gonna be such a crowd pleaser?"

"I had a feeling," I said. "Are you gonna rinse, dude? You've been brushing for a while."

"Nah, man, I'm just thorough."

There hadn't been that much alcohol in our evening. Perhaps we were just slaphappy. Or, simply, happy.

The Invitation

I bumped into my mom's boss at the grocery store on a Sunday. It was the week of my birthday. I stood in the aisle near the expensive cheeses, thick bacon, and pre-prepared meals. That's where Joe noticed me.

"Scott, I've been thinking about calling you. We're having a book club tomorrow night."

"Oh really? What about?"

"It's about an anthropologist who spent time in Venezuela. I know you're doing the linguistics training so I figured it'd be good to invite you."

"Oh wow, thanks."

"Yeah, he'll be there, too—the anthropologist. Maybe you guys'll have something in common."

"Maybe. But to be honest…" I hesitated to say what was next, not knowing if it would reveal too much— "Christians and anthropologists have not always seen eye to eye."

I knew this because I had taken an anthropology class taught by a Christian and missionary. Towards the end of the term she devoted an entire class period to the relationships between missionaries and anthropologists. She said that in the early days, missionaries headed to the field were advised to get to know the secular anthropologists living in the area. And vice-versa, anthropologists might benefit from getting to know the missionaries in the areas they served. But over time, this relationship crumbled, to the point where a film called *War of the Gods* got Christian missionaries kicked out of Colombia. At least, that was the claim advanced by another Christian anthropology professor as he showed us the film for extra credit one afternoon.

"They got us good," he said, pausing the film at halftime. "And it's about to get worse." The film was created by a few British anthropologists who had gone to live among and film a tribal group in the Amazon. At the same time, they spent some time filming the nearby missionaries. One scene shows the anthropologists in loincloths joining the tribesmen in a river, trapping fish. Another scene shows children from the tribe in class at a Catholic boarding school. A nun is up at the chalkboard writing the word *sin*, giving an uneasy look at the camera. It was sleight of hand, according to the professor showing the film. To English-speaking viewers, "Oh, what horrible indoctrination, teaching these poor kids about sin." However, upon reflection, this was Colombia, and the word '*sin*' in Spanish simply meant, "without." Would the editors stoop so low as to inserting such a misleading scene into the film? Wouldn't it be worth it to just present the subjects in an honest, even-handed light?

Needless to say, there was a contentious history between anthropologists and Christians. This is why it took me a moment to think about what I might be agreeing to in joining the book club.

"Anyway," Joe said, "you probably won't have time to read the whole book. But feel free to join us. I'll text you the address."

I was flattered. A grown-up was inviting me to a grown-up event. He even thought I might have something to contribute.

The next day at school, I printed out a profile piece about the author from the New York Times. I did not have time to read his book, but I might have time to make it through the article and acquaint myself with the man. I also shot out a text to a missionary friend who had lived in Venezuela.

"Have you heard of Reginald Johnson?"

"Yeah, he's got quite a reputation."

"Oh yeah? How so?"

"He lived in the area near one of the other families in the organization. There were reports of nefarious activities."

"Sounds juicy. Well I may be attending a book club tonight where he is the featured speaker."

"That sounds like quite an opportunity.

"Yeah, would you be able to email me a little about your time there? Just so I might have something related to contribute?"

"Sure, just let me know what you want."

I worked on an email for him.

Jim,

Thanks so much for your prayer and thoughts.

1. When/how long were you with the Ninam?

2. How comparable are they to the Yanomami?

3. What would you say were the positives and negatives of the Ninam culture? What did they teach you? What did they reveal to you about yourself, and American culture?

4. In what ways would you say the presence of missionaries such as yourself changed the culture?

I recalled something Jim had once told me about population estimates. There was something about the tribe's declining numbers going back up when he and the other missionary families lived among them. Something perhaps to do with a rabbit project providing more protein. I also recalled that Jim and his family, along with all other missionaries were kicked out due to a decree from Chavez. They were given ninety days to pack up and get out. The soldiers that took over burned what remained of their belongings.

At the bottom of the email I included a link to an article I had read before. It was from an atheist columnist for *The Times* in London, "As an atheist I truly believe Africa needs God." It was something I thought Jim would appreciate.

I knew the potential critiques of Christian or missionary presence among indigenous groups. Did they destroy cultures? Did they impose Christianity over against the traditional beliefs of a people? Did they impose Western values and essentially set up a springboard for a capitalist swindle? I wanted to be prepared to share the positives I had heard.

The year before, a study came out that linked missionary efforts to democracy and improved life outcomes. "Conversionary protestants" truly desired that the peoples convert to Christianity, and they emphasized literacy and education in order for people to be able to read the Scriptures. This led to engaged civic participation and democracy. The results could be seen today. In Togo, where missionaries were limited, the university had paltry resources dating back to the 1960s and 70s. Meanwhile, in Ghana, where British missionaries had established a system of schools and printing presses, the university library was full and education was flourishing. The results of the study had been popularized in *Christianity Today.*

I started my research into Johnson. The New York Times article mentioned that there had been an academic controversy between him and other professors. It had to do with whether the tribe with whom he lived was truly a violent, fierce people. It sounded a little racist on the face of it, but then again, he had actually lived among them and been through quite a bit of violence.

I was not sure I understood it all completely, but the thrust of the Johnson's latest book was that he had been misrepresented. Academia was its own minefield, but then there were interactions with government authorities and neighboring missionaries. The controversies even spilled over into the newspapers, becoming common knowledge for the mainstream. And thus, Joe's book club had picked it up for discussion.

I debated over what I should wear to the event. I didn't want to be too dressed up. But also not too dressed down. I decided to go with jeans—what I probably would have worn anyway.

I drove south of town, praying as I went. I had asked for prayer from Jim, too.

"What an opportunity!" he told me over the phone.

"Yeah, but what if he's mean?"

"He needs God just like you and I do."

I parked my car on the street in a remote wooded area south of town. I walked up to the house which was way nicer on the inside than I expected. By the time I made my way to the bathroom, I noticed that the man hosting the party had monogrammed towels in the bathroom. The only other time I had seen this was on my financial advisor's shirt cuff.

I walked into the kitchen and saw Joe standing next to Johnson at the island counter. He was sitting on a bar stool with an oxygen tank nearby, and the tubing hooked up to his nose. Somehow, he looked strong.

"Scott, I'm glad you could make it!" Joe introduced me to Reginald. "This is Scott, he's studying linguistics in… which school is it again?"

"The University of North Dakota," I said. Johnson appeared disarmed. I think he had been preparing himself for someone studying with SIL—the Summer Institute of Linguistics. It was true, I was, but the very name would raise eyebrows given their history in South America—what with being kicked out of Colombia. SIL had worked out a partnership with the University of North Dakota. So that's what I chose to reveal in my introduction.

"Oh," Johnson said. "Nice to meet you."

The spread was nice. Joe offered me a beer. There were cans and bottles on ice from the local breweries. But I wanted to be in top shape for this. There was a cheese tray, with one of those knives with a divot on the end. *This is big time*, I thought. I walked into the nearby living room where I recognized some of my mom's other coworkers. Ivan the IT guy, who was also the father of one of my students, and William, a friend of my dad's. They introduced me to a man who was a professor of anthropology at a nearby college. Perhaps he would be the best equipped to take down the author if it came to controversy.

At the same time, I imagined that everyone in the room was there to hear what I might have to say. I had printed out the email response Jim had sent me, thinking I might have something to share. I wanted this to be a significant evening.

I took a seat next to Ivan in the room where we'd be having the discussion. He was a shield between me and the author, who was a few seats in the circle to my right. Body odor arose from the man to my left— whom I assume had worked harder and made more money than me that day.

Johnson spoke in a gruff, powerful voice. It seemed to reflect a lifetime of being harassed and contradicted by peers. On the one hand, if a man can survive in the rainforest for years at a time, he deserves some respect for just being able to do what most people can't, or wouldn't dare. On the other hand, if he had acted unethically or had misrepresented people, then those things ought to be revealed, I thought—at least, in an appropriate way, and at an appropriate time.

There was a mention of a measles outbreak in the tribe he had lived among. This was one of the ongoing accusations. That he, or someone else, had been a part of bringing measles into this unvaccinated population, which resulted in the deaths of hundreds. The Times article had alluded to it without passing judgment. Then someone in the circle took a stab at the culprit.

"It was the evangelicals," said the large man sitting to my left. He said it with a harrumph. Johnson did not confirm it, but he left it open to interpretation. At the very least, as far as Johnson was concerned, it was not his fault. The group's momentary silence seemed to disclose the consensus. *Yep, evangelicals are the bad guys, like always. Forcing their religion on others, and then bringing measles into a vulnerable community. What will they do next?*

I hadn't read enough to weigh in on the question. How would I know the inner workings of a situation on a different continent? Still, I felt a need to act. Was I the only one in the circle for whom the word 'evangelical' didn't automatically have the connotation of 'criminal'? I did not like the word myself, but I felt like something needed to be corrected.

Then the mention of missionary kids came up. Johnson recounted a time when he saw missionary kids on the organization's compound, standing at the edge of the jungle, looking in with trepidation. Everyone chuckled at the thought of their naïveté. I wanted to weigh in.

"It seems like you've been through a lot," I said. He looked in my direction.

"You've been misrepresented by all kinds of groups." He looked at me, surprised that I had something to say. "And that's the thing I wouldn't want for anybody, to be misrepresented." It was going to be an Oscar-winning moment.

"As it happens, one of my friends lived in Venezuela. He sent me an update from some missionary friends that lived in the rainforest." I pulled up my printed out email.

"Where'd you get that? Who is that?" the author asked. It was like in *A River Wild* when Meryl Streep and her son break out sign language to foil their kidnappers.

I continued.

"My friend lived with a group called the Ninam. I'm not sure how far they were from the group you lived with, but he said they have some similar language."

"Ninam!" Johnson said. "No one has called the group by that name in years!" There was a guffaw in the room, especially from the man who had earlier harrumphed.

I sensed that I was being discredited before I had a chance. I longed to share Jim's appreciation of the culture. To show that missionaries do respect and learn from the people they live with. But I was not getting a chance to share any of this. I rushed to address the thought of missionary kids being afraid of the people living in the jungle.

"That may be the case for some," I said, "but my friend's friend's family here married into the tribe they were living with."

There was a silence. Maybe it was too many degrees of separation, but it was having an impact. At this point the weight in the room seemed to lean back on me. It was escalating, and I had played a part.

Johnson took the reins again. "I remember how much of a pain some of them were," he said, referring to a missionary family that lived nearby. They had come up with a large, painted drawing, showing the people in the tribe walking up to a big cliff, and nearly off the other side, like lemmings.

"*Turn from your ways!* they told the people. *When you drink and do drugs and have these parties, you are worshipping demons!* they told them." Johnson had our attention.

"Well, I had had about enough of this," he said. "So I went out there right in the middle of where they were talking and said, *You know what, everybody? I say tonight we bring out the beer and the drugs and get as messed up as we want, worshipping these demons!*" Then I turned to the missionary family and said, *Fuuuuuck you!*" He raised his middle finger and showed it in a semi-arc for our group, a 180-degree *Exorcist* spin.

I smiled an uneasy smile. The rest of the circle laughed. What was at stake here, really?

I listened for the rest of the talk. The other anthropology professor gave a brief challenge concerning one of the evolutionary biology claims, but it was getting late.

After the book circle dispersed, the author made his way to the bathroom. William, from the other end of the circle, got my attention.

"So you know people that are translating the Bible out there?" he asked.

"Yeah, not this family personally, but others in other parts of the world."

"That's amazing," he said.

"Yeah, they always have great stories." I went into one.

"My friend who was in Venezuela talks about being in the back of the canoe when a giant anaconda fell right into their boat. He told the tribesman in the front of the boat, 'I could use your machete, we've got a snake situation.' The man in the front of the boat said, 'Ah, that's just a tree trunk.' My friend said, 'Okay, well, can I have your machete to take care of this tree situation?' He grabbed the machete and tried to chop the anaconda, but he said it was like hitting steel. The blade just ricocheted off. And while he was telling this story, another friend from Guyana, who didn't say a lot, chimed in, 'You have to aim for the eye.'"

The author emerged from the bathroom to hear the rest of the story.

"That's right," he said. "They're mean mothers."

An opening. Even if I'd bumbled the discussion, we might be able to talk now. I joined the rest of the men in the kitchen again, where they scooped the rest of the cheese onto crackers. They discussed the author's temporary office location north of town.

"Do you have any free time this week that I might come by for a visit?" I asked Johnson.

"Why?" he said. It was one of the most forceful *why*'s I had ever heard.

"I don't know, just to keep talking." It was a longshot. I regretted it as soon as I'd said it.

On the drive home, a thought came to me. *That would have showed him*. I imagined having a re-go at it. The painting was the sticking point. How horrible, a missionary family telling the tribe they were going to hell with a feltboard. How apparently noble, on the other hand, an anthropologist joining in their celebrations and letting them be.

But what if the painting was not a scolding, but an invitation? An abrasive, gruff invitation—but an invitation still. And Johnson's was simply another invitation—to keep doing drugs. It was dueling invitations—the story of our evening.

Salsa

It was an excuse for us to get close to girls. At least that was how my roommate Aaron verbalized it. I hadn't thought things that far through, nor did I have the courage to say it. But when you've got a partner, improvisation flows and eventually you've come up with something beautiful.

Aaron and I sat in the living room of the house we had inherited from my brother. Aaron and I had been roommates since undergrad, and when he returned to Mizzou for grad school, my older brother had bequeathed to us his house.

"Just be nice to the neighbors," he said.

One of Aaron's Friday night habits in grad school was to rent a DVD and watch it the same night. Shia Labeouf's *Lawless* comes to mind, a Prohibition-era tale where he tries to win a church girl. We finished the movie and sat in the dark.

"What are you going to do with your Friday nights, now?" Aaron asked. It was a good question. For the past few years I had volunteered leading Bible discussion groups for international students on campus. We would meet, eat, sing songs, and then break off into small groups for Bible story discussion. Due to a variety of circumstances, I realized I did not need to continue in the ministry.

"Good question," I said. "There's the thesis I could be working on, but I do that Wednesdays and Saturdays. Friday night would be good for a break."

"Correct. And what could we devote all these Fridays to?"

I was vaguely aware that Latin dancing occurred every weekend downtown. I had walked by multiple times, never having the skills or courage to go in myself. It just sounded lively, and I was locked out.

"I guess we could try salsa," I said.

"Bingo," Aaron said.

"There's just one thing though," I said, easing my way into the subject. "Often when Jesus did miracles, he would tell the people not to go and tell anyone."

"So you're saying?"

"I'm saying let's keep it quiet. We don't need to go telling everyone."

"You're equating your dancing with Jesus' ministry, great."

My initial experience with dancing had been a horror, a dread. Around age 14, my parents enrolled me, as they had my brother before me, into cotillion. It was a production hosted in one of the town's elementary school gymnasiums — where each weekend we were taught to dance. Ballroom, country, and swing. The most horrifying thing was trying to pick a partner. Over the weeks I developed a few acquaintances I could turn to, but they were matches of desperation and convenience. Each week before going I prayed to God for a way out. In my teen study Bible I would look up, "fear" and try to find some answers. But it never got me out of actually going.

Years later, at prom, I had a partner, and one dance move. I would bob my shoulders back and forth, left and right. A friend would say of me afterwards, "Scott, you don't know how to dance, but you were getting down."

So I would learn.

The next Friday night after Aaron and I committed to learning salsa, we entered The Blue Fugue, a quaint bar with a busted up wooden floor and bookshelves lining the walls. Some sat at the bar and at the booths in the back. I had once been in here on a Sunday afternoon to watch Spain play Germany in the EuroCup. It was all dudes for that get-together. Now I would be interacting with actual, authentic ladies.

We stood mingling waiting for the instruction to begin. It was a lesson from 9-10pm, then a round of shots at 10pm, followed by an open dance floor.

Our instructors were a slim male engineering student wearing all black, and a female lead with killer hair who was working as a server at a restaurant in town. They faced the stage and instructed us in the salsa basic step. *1, 2, 3, 5, 6, 7.* The 4 and 8 counts were rests. After a little of this we were to partner off. Aaron gave me a nudge by asking a girl and her friend if they'd be our partners. He had led the way in asking and all I had to do was follow. They were also pretty much the only two ladies available. It was much easier than trying to find someone in a gym full of people.

The instructors demonstrated how to do the steps with a partner— how to hold hands, at what angle our elbows should be, how much tension there should be. They didn't specify how much sweat should be on our palms.

They went over the open position and closed position— the latter bringing you into closer contact with your partner with your hand on her back. I had touched the back of a girl in cotillion, but it had been about a decade. Tonight, however, we were grown ups, and everything was in a safe environment as long as the instructors were still shepherding us.

They taught us the cross-body lead, where you and your partner would exchange places, 180 degrees. They taught us how to spin the girl, making sure to signal her on the *1,2,3* counts by lightly squeezing her palm or raising her right arm.

From there, it wasn't too difficult. Our steps for the evening were to arrive, ask someone to dance, and dance. Then repeat. It was easier to dance with girls who were new to salsa. Usually the professionals wouldn't give us the time of day.

Aaron pulled me aside one crowded evening.

"Two new girls just showed up," he told me, meeting me underneath a loft where the stereo equipment was held. "Sarah and Emily," he said. "Sarah, I must say, has a very strong grip. Emily— super hot."

They made their way over to us and split off. I danced with Emily. She was slim with long black curly hair and blue eyes, wearing a white cashmere shawl of some sort. We stayed in the open position, and I counted for her as we did the steps, *1,2,3,5,6,7*. She looked down at her feet and smiled, just going with the rhythm, mesmerized. It was an ideal moment for me as a teacher. Normally on Friday nights I would be leading students through the life of Jesus, but here I was leading a single girl, amongst others, through the basic step.

Aaron later danced with a partner who was a little more flirtatious.

"You know the best thing about the basic position?" she told him.

"What's that?" he asked.

"It's the perfect setup for *grinding*."

"Let's save room for Jesus," Aaron replied.

Quickly, we learned that we needed some distinguishing moves— shines. This way, it wasn't just the basic step for the duration of the song. Aaron had a move where after spinning the girl, he'd duck under her arm and spin himself. I was impressed with his quick innovation. I borrowed it. But I was hungry for more.

I searched YouTube to find more shines to incorporate. I lighted on Franklin Diaz, a professional dancer who wasn't afraid to be goofy. His dancing told a story. It was like Play-Doh. My favorite clip of Diaz was shot with a green night-vision lens. He would beckon his partner close, and then playfully push her away. Then again, beckon her close, and push her away. Then on the third time, he would beckon her close and embrace her, to her delight, and the delight of all around. This was what I wanted to do.

I developed a ritual on Friday nights before going. Changing my socks, brushing my teeth, and putting my jeans in the dryer for a few minutes, for a tighter fit.

I became familiar with the playlists from repeated exposure. Every night started out with Oscar D'Leon "Llorarás." Then it was Prince Royce for bachata. The song "Ámame O Déjame" by Kevin Ceballo became a favorite of mine for salsa. Then the live band, La Movida, would take the stage. Their song "Cumanchero" was for merengue, where I learned to just march and take my partner through loops with my arms in the air.

As we became regulars, we got to know the cast of characters. There was a tall redheaded guy who often wore suspenders and a hat. He had flirtatious hat trick he would do. While sticking with the basic step, he would place the hat on his partner for a moment, do a flirty face, and then retrieve his hat. We hated him for it.

Elizabeth, our main friend on Friday nights, informed us that the redheaded guy was a chef in town. He had invited her to breakfast on occasion. We thought this was as risqué as his hat move. Did art mimic life? Was he promiscuous? We may have been there to dance, but we couldn't help doing a lot of judging, too.

One Saturday evening, Aaron and I sat at the bar at Addison's waiting for Elizabeth to join us.

Elizabeth arrived and we moved to a booth. A chessboard was set up. Aaron began to sing songs from *The Lion King* while I narrated matter of factly.

"This is why I love you guys," she said. "You're so different." She explained that she had been invited to Déjà Vu to dance later that evening. It would not be salsa, and given my experience at that bar, it would not be wholesome.

"Elizabeth, I do not want you going to that den of sin!" Aaron insisted.

One night, upon discovering a shared appreciation for *Fiddler on the Roof*, Elizabeth invited us to her brother's house to watch it. We obliged.

We made our way to his large house where he lived with his family. He worked as an engineer. The combination of his career path and the size of his house felt like we were stepping into the unknown of intimidating success. But he was inviting like a teddy bear when we arrived. There was no question of, "What are you doing hanging out with my sister?" Aaron and I came as a duo, so the threat was neutralized.

Aaron and I were both involved in religious ministries in town. Eventually, the word spread that we were dancing, and others wanted to join.

I stood in the kitchen of Joanna's house after our church small group meeting. I mentioned that I was getting into salsa dancing.

"That's great. I bet you've good at it," Tara said. I was flattered, but didn't ask why she thought I'd be good. Was it my svelte figure? My background in skateboarding that would give me core balance on the dance floor? Or was there something dancer-y about my personality?

Years before, when I had taken the OKCupid test, the result I received was the Slow Dancer— "Steady, reliable, cradling her tenderly. Take a deep breath, and let it out real easy… you are **The Slow Dancer.**" The profile continued, "Your focus is love, not sex, and for your age, you have average experience. But you're a great, thoughtful guy, and your love life improves every year."

Perhaps my personality was coming to life. At least my dancing skills were. One Friday I asked one of the more advanced dancers to dance. She had a good sense of humor, but I was still slightly intimidated because she danced with the best guys. Plus, she wore her jeans really well.

We went to the middle of the dance floor and I spun her as usual, but this time I continued holding onto her left hand behind her back for something called a hammer lock. It was an intermediate move, and it always set your partner up for something more.

"You're getting better," she told me with her eyes. *What are you going to do next?* Was the implication.

One Friday evening at The Blue Fugue, it started out with one other girl from my small group. Aaron was not there. Just me and her, waiting for the dancing to start. I thought of what a friend had told me who had lived in the Middle East, where interaction between the sexes was closely monitored. "Whenever an unmarried man and unmarried woman are alone, they are not alone. Satan is there." I had not thought of this particular girl standing next to me as a love interest— but was she interested in me? Did she see romance in dance, where I saw fun?

Shortly thereafter, others from our church small groups showed up— Luke, Christina, Frank, and Karen and Michelle. It felt like a family party. We formed a circle and Michelle had us laughing with her rendition of "the Coke machine" dance— where she pantomimed inserting a dollar into a vending machine, and then pounding against it rhythmically upon not receiving her drink.

The male dance instructor took a liking to Christina, she reported to us after their dance.

"He asked me where I was from. I told him Georgia. He put his hand on my chin and said, 'You could be my Georgia peach.'" We all had a laugh standing outside The Blue Fugue. Now we were the ones spilling out into the street, radiating double joy as dancers and Christ followers. If only those passing by knew how much fun was to be had on the inside.

When it was time to go home, we walked down 9th street to the Heidelberg. Some girls from a sorority were collecting donations in coffee cans.

"You know," I told the group, "last week I was walking with Aaron downtown and he told the women collecting money in cans that their fundraising approach was boring. That they needed to do more, to really earn it. He suggested they should dance. I was like, 'Aaron, I don't feel good about telling women to do stuff so that I will then pay them for watching. That's something that happens in a different kind of club.'" The group had a laugh.

We found a booth for all of us to fit in. Luke and Karen were staffers for campus student ministries. Then Christina and Frank were grad students in Psychology. Christina and Karen sat across from me while I hinted at a personal problem.

"What do you do if someone wants to hang out with you too much, and you don't want to hang out with them?"

"Boundaries are good," Christina said. I went on for a while, not naming names or getting into specifics. Then it became clear that I was indirectly referring to a girl.

"Oh," Karen said, "It's a girl." Apparently, that changed everything. She had plenty of experience counseling students during one-on-one meetings on campus. I trusted their opinions. These were my sisters.

"I can tell that this is weighing heavily on you," Christina commented, noticing that my demeanor had changed quite a bit since dancing. They were there for me, supporting me in all of life.

About the same time, Aaron made a friend at Hillel, the Jewish student organization. She became a regular on Friday nights. She wore all black, with bright red lipstick. I took a dance with her while Aaron took a break.

"So how much hip is too much hip, for a man, when I'm dancing?" I asked her, trying to joke.

"I'd say keep it subtle. But hey, you do you," she said. She was calm and collected, and definitely smarter than me. We bonded over the shared experience of Friday nights, of being tired and wanting to sleep, yet knowing that if we went out dancing it'd be so much fun.

She lived in an apartment not far from us, which she rented out to a guest through Air BnB. She asked if she could spend the night at our place, and we did have an extra bed. I introduced her to my shampoos.

"Anything you need in the morning, it's right here," I said. "Nothing touches this body but pure coconut."

"Oh interesting," she said. "You really do have all coconut shampoos and conditioners."

With her AirBnB guest over to our house, we watched an action movie set in Germany. Now we had become the givers of hospitality, in a bizarro twenty-something reversal of what Elizabeth's brother had done for us.

A few weeks later, I noticed Aaron looking dejected.

"What's going on?" I asked him.

"She said she wanted a relationship with me."

"Whoa. How did you respond?"

"I said I couldn't provide that for her right now, with all the stuff I've got going on."

"That's rough."

I was blown away. Instead of just being bachelors, we had now become eligible. It had all happened right underneath our noses, without us expecting it. We were in the prime of our lives, but were holding back from commitment.

I had also reached a plateau in my dancing skills. Whether salsa or bachata, the only way I could imagine going further was by getting closer—socially and physically. If I ever wanted to pull off a 360 cross body lead, I would need to have devoted time with a particular partner to practice.

I watched a professional couple one Friday night who had come in from St. Louis. The male dancer wore black pants that flared out at the bottom, and a wide open shirt that exposed what would have been chest hair. His partner wore a short skirt that lifted when she spun. To watch them dance was like watching a double helix. They were in tune with each other, fluid, hands all over. I would not be able to pull this off without an actual girlfriend. And though I now had the courage to ask almost any girl to dance, I did not think to ask anyone out.

In the springtime, I tried to think about what I might give up for Lent. After some prayer, it hit me— salsa. There was nothing wrong with dancing, but if I had to admit what had occupied and filled my life for the past few months, it would be salsa. It was like tasting God, having the thing I'd give up for Lent come to me. Direction for temporary renunciation.

Meanwhile, I bumped into a female friend of friend at Shiloh Bar & Grill. My friends and I sat at a round table facing the TV, where the NBA Slam Dunk Contest was airing. A lone guitarist in the opposite corner of the room struggled to keep our attention. My friend ordered me a gin & tonic— the grown up Sprite. Then his friend Heather showed up. Having an actual girl in our presence, our backs straightened. Through my months of salsa dancing and co-ed small group interactions, I had been prepared. I learned that Heather and I had gone to the same high school, and that we both loved musical theatre. I told her I worked at another high school, and often had tickets to shows. She said to let her know when the next show was coming up, and gave me her number.

It was *School House Rock*, the same show that had been put on when we were in high school. I texted her and arranged for us to meet there. She showed up right as the show was starting, wearing a sweater with a collared shirt underneath it.

We found our seats, but as the show rolled on, we were unimpressed. At intermission, near the table of candy and treats, she asked me if I wanted to call an audible and head to Flat Branch. Improvisation. It felt like the right thing to do.

At the restaurant we were ushered to a table where we sat elbow to elbow at the corner, rather than across from each other as in an actual date. We talked neurology and ordered pretzels and dip. I learned that she was Catholic, and I mentioned that I had given up salsa for Lent.

"You're a dancer?" she said. "I had no idea. But why give up salsa for lent? There's nothing wrong with it."

"Right. But it's like it had dominated my life for a while, and I wanted to see if I still loved God without it."

"Interesting," she replied.

I returned home and found Aaron in the living room.

"How was the show?" he asked.

"Unimpressive. We left at halftime and went to Flat Branch."

"Really? Who was she?" We pulled out his laptop do so some quick Facebook stalking so I could identify her for him.

"You had a friend date!" he erupted.

"I suppose I did." If our goal had been to get close to girls, I had done it.

All were invited. And yet, to toot our own horns, only a few had actually gone in for the risk— an encounter with the Other, even multiple others, in a single night.

Take an empty Friday night, an empty dance floor, a smattering of bored people, and breathe life into it all with music and dance. This was the way life was supposed to be, and we had been there to taste it.

The Barber

It was my first time to the opera, and I was underdressed. Ali pointed it out to me in the parking garage.

"You're going to wear that?" he asked. Somehow he was already always well dressed. He was from Central Asia, with family in Italy. He was a year or two older than me and had a taste for the finer things. He could have passed for European— the accent, the tan skin, dark hair, short trunks at the swimming pool.

I pulled a collared plaid shirt out of the my trunk, along with some dressier looking shoes a friend had given me. I kept my socks on. I couldn't pull off the sockless look Ali pulled off casually. I would end up with blisters or sweating feet.

It was *The Barber of Seville*, one I would recognize from Bugs Bunny cartoons. Going into the Lyric Opera of Kansas City was like going into a spaceship, except that there were tuxedos sprinkled in. Ali ordered a drink at the bar and I ordered a Twix bar— another giveaway that I was out of my element. As soon as I gave my tip, I realized it was insufficient. I didn't realize that a $2 candy bar would appropriately entail a $5 tip. The bartender turned her back on me.

We took our seats up in the grand tier left ring. A single man sat to our left. He was a regular. The orchestra tuned their instruments in the pit. I recalled that a friend living in Kansas City had mentioned how much the city was pushing the arts. Just a month before I had been there to see *Sweeney Todd*. They served mincemeat pies at intermission. In the playbill that was handed out was an advertisement for the coming opera— "Meet the real barber." So I decided to go for it.

It turned out I wasn't the only one being pulled in. The opera was definitely drawing in regulars. The man to my left had driven in from a small town in Kansas. Opera may have been an acquired taste, but people were getting on board with it.

The performance began. We recognized the overture. The lyrics were subtitled for us on the balcony railing. I alternated between reading and gazing below at the brightly colored production. There was even a man on stilts. Then the barber himself came out— Figaro, with the aria we are familiar with. The translation scrolled for me.

Ah, what a life, what a pleasure
For a barber of quality!
... A more noble life cannot be found.

I had always heard the part where he says "Figaro" multiple times, without understanding the rest of the song. Apparently this was a man who loved life, and someone whom everyone was calling on for help or a haircut.

It was amazing to see the barber personified, and then kept in context for the rest of the story. The actor who played Figaro wore a beard and long curly hair, like I imagined Ali's would be if he grew it out. But he kept it closely cropped, as he did mine.

The Monday before, Ali offered to cut my hair for the first time. I was apprehensive.

"Have you cut hair before?" I asked.

"Sure, all the time," he reassured me. "It'll be fine. Don't worry about it." I heard the same tone from lazy students who promised to eventually get around to their homework.

I arrived at Ali's apartment and he took me out to the cement porch. He cleared away the grill and brought out a chair from his living room. It was a stretch for the extension cord with the clippers—but he made it work.

"Now take off your shirt." We were getting close. I did not want to have to expose myself to the neighbors, but this was Ali's place and I wanted to be in the element. He turned on music from his country on his phone to complete the experience. The only thing that was missing was a hookah.

"You have a lot more hair on the sides of your head that on the top," he said. "It's the same with me."

We were getting older. I had just hit 30. We were ushered into the 30 Somethings singles' group at church, where we first met.

"If you have a thousand hairs on the top, I've probably got 700," he told me. He spoke of his desire to get hair implants when he was older, if he had the money. It seemed like a vain pursuit to me, but he looked good. Ali was always edging me up one notch ahead in style and culture, like with the settings on the electric clippers.

In February, our Tuesday night small group meeting had fallen on my birthday. I had just given blood at school, so my legs were a little shaky when we met at my co-leader's house. Still, I had resolved to share a short writing with the group. I wanted to tell the story of my friend's wedding, and how that same day had given me the resolve to remain single. I felt the need to communicate this message clearly to our small group, which was co-ed, so that no one would be disappointed when I didn't want to date them.

The Monday following this meeting, I met with Ali at Moe's for burritos.

"Are you sure you want to stay single for your whole life?" he asked me as we sat in a red pleather booth. "I mean, maybe now it's all right, but what about when you get older? Don't you worry that you won't have anyone to hang out with?"

It was a little sensitive, but I was glad he had asked me. I launched into my spiel about how Jesus promises hundreds of brothers and sisters in the present age for anyone who leaves home or family for his sake and the sake of the good news. If this was a promise from Jesus, I could trust him for people to hang out with in my 40's and 50's, though I rarely thought that far ahead. I also failed to admit that in the passage referenced, Jesus did not mention giving up a wife. I also failed to realize that I hadn't exactly left my home for the sake of the gospel. I was still in Columbia.

Yet for the time being I did have people to hang out with, including Ali at Moe's. We realized we had a shared love of reading.

"Sometimes in the evening," he said, "when I'm finished with my school work. I will pick up a novel or some poetry, and just take my time with it. Maybe read a little, then just reflect on it for a while. Maybe pour some wine, and just enjoy it."

I had to admit, it was a pretty classy way to spend an evening.

The hope of opening up and being transparent was that others in the small group would be, too. *Transparency begets transparency*, perhaps, was the axiom I was going off of. The Monday before we went to the opera in April, Ali invited me to his apartment to play pool. I waited for him in the evening in the lobby, where everything was dark. He came out of his apartment with a friend who was just leaving, then Ali and I moved to his room.

He had a story to share. He sat on the couch while I sat on a leather chair nearby. It was like our own personal small group. He opened up about his predicament in the States. When he studied in the Middle East, he became disaffected with the country's majority religion. Some individuals close to him forced him to pray. He explained that they considered it an infection if anyone did not go along with the majority religion.

Meanwhile, he recalled a day visiting a church that was open for prayer. He spoke with a cleric and felt welcomed. At home and work, he continued to do the forced prayers of the majority religion, but hated every moment of it.

Moving to the States, he one day while biking stumbled across the church I attended. He spoke of the same feeling of comfort and welcome. In Handel's *Messiah* the song is "He shall feed his flock like a shepherd, and he shall carry the lambs with his arms." The image of Jesus carrying sheep was an ancient one, inscribed on catacomb walls, and Ali was apparently finding this same comfort. He spoke of meeting with one of the pastors and being baptized.

Then he explained his fears of going back home. A relative of his had recently been stabbed for becoming a

Christian. He did not want the same thing to happen to himself. And so he requested from me a letter for his asylum application. As the small group leader, I might be able to testify to his history of attendance to our meetings.

I said I'd do it.

I wrote the letter that week, rounding it out with the following closing:

I am very glad that the pastor placed Ali in our small group. I am not in a position to judge hearts, but I do not doubt the sincerity of Ali's desire to follow Jesus and be a part of his people. I am glad he is in our group in Columbia and I am glad to call him a friend.

That Thursday, I invited Ali out to my parent's house to give him the letter. The weather was nice, so we sat on the screened-in porch with lemonade. He read over the letter and made some edits. I had gone a little heavy on the bro vibe, and he imagined the person we were submitting the letter to would be more interested in his evidence of actually becoming a Christian and needing asylum.

After going over the letter, I also handed him a translation of the Song of Solomon in a language he was familiar with. A missionary friend had given it to me. I got out my phone to record the audio of Ali reading it. I couldn't believe that things had seemingly come full circle. I had desired to leave my home for the sake of sharing the good news with the nations, but it hadn't worked out. And yet, God had brought someone into my life in need, and I had a part to play in it.

We went to the bank to get the letter notarized. Then we swung by Fretboard Coffee where there was a poetry reading during the literary festival in town. We sat outside the coffee shop for a moment while he showed me photos on his phone. He had been to Puerto Rico with a former girlfriend, beaming and wearing pastels. *Can a man just up and do that?* I wondered. *Did he sleep with her?* I wondered. *Was this before or after he had started following Jesus?* I did not intend to coerce him, but I was concerned.

We stood in the back of the coffee shop as the poetry reading began. I couldn't help but notice that he was subtly interacting with the young woman standing near us. It was like he just had constant game. I wondered if that would make following Jesus difficult. For my part, I had attempted to suppress most of it in myself, reasoning that I did not want to lead any girls on. I didn't know how or whether I should attempt to speak into a new Christian's life about girls. But perhaps I was leaving something undone.

The night of the opera after the opera, Ali requested that I drop him off at his friend's apartment. I learned that he had not made reservations for me. I felt slighted. Weren't we in this together? Brothers bonding with high art? Why part afterwards? I called a friend in Kansas City who was able to put me on his couch for the night.

The next morning, I drove back to his friend's apartment to pick him up. Ali made one request over the phone, "And please remember not to mention anything about church, okay?" My heart sank. It was an uncomfortable request. Wasn't Ali happy to be a Christian? What would hold him back from letting his friends know? I did not want to force him into confessing anything, but hadn't I testified to his devotion?

The plan was to bring Ali's friend back with us to Columbia. We stopped at *Paleterias Tropicanas*, a Mexican popsicle stand. The items were delicious, and I recorded on my phone the audio of Ali and his friend's admiration of the popsicles— English mixed with a language from Ali's country. We took home extras with us in the trunk to share with others.

It turned out that that same Saturday, Ali was going to be in a play on campus in afternoon. I was blown away. He was living all of life. It was as if he exuded cool. He invited me to the show.

I sat near the front. Two other plays went first, then his. He stood in the center of the stage with his interlocutor. They talked about his lover, and it was gradually revealed on the big screen in the back that his lover was a goat. It was simple yet brilliant. He had us laughing, daydreaming about his goat.

I congratulated him after the show, and he was off to hang out with his friends. I am not sure what I expected, but I couldn't help but feel abandoned for the second night in a row.

During one of our small group meetings at my house, before I knew about Ali's predicament, I spoke about longevity. We were going through the letter of 1st Peter in the Bible, one where he writes to Christians facing persecution. I mentioned how longevity was not a guarantee for any Christian. I spoke of Martin Luther King, Jr. and Dietrich Bonhoeffer, whom I considered to be members of the 39 Club for their early deaths. Ali sat silently in a chair against the wall of my living room. I had not realized what he might actually be facing.

And yet after the opera and trip back to Columbia, I wanted him to treasure Jesus more. You can't force anyone to pray, but what about reminding them of everything they've got access to in Christ? I wanted him to not be ashamed of the good news about Jesus. And I wanted him to not be ashamed of me. I wanted him to realize he had an inheritance, a guaranteed resurrection, and brothers and sisters across the globe, of whom I wanted to be one.

For Spring Break, I took a trip to visit a friend in Texas. He was a missionary near Ali's home country. I thought of inviting Ali, and listening to Bonhoeffer's *The Cost of Discipleship* on the way there, but I ended up driving alone and listening to *Life Together.*

I returned to Columbia for a haircut from Ali. We met at my house this time, setting up a straight backed chair in the middle of the living room's hardwood floor. It would be my job to sweep up the hair afterwards, but the floors made it easy. Before starting the haircut, I couldn't help but notice Ali's noticing the young woman across the street mowing her yard.

"What does she think she's doing in those shoes?" he asked, biting his fingernail. She was wearing slip-on shoes, trying to mow down a slope.

"I don't know," I said, trying not to pay attention, "mowing, I guess."

He began to cut my hair and spoke of his brother, back home.

"I'd like for him to come here," he said. "And I'd like him to be able to practice English, before he gets here. Do you think you'd be able to help him?"

I had learned from experience that I did not like teaching English. I always preferred to learn the other person's language. In this case, I did not want to get roped into an activity of which I was not sure of the payoff. What were the odds that he'd actually make it to the States? And if he did, he would have plenty of English practice here.

"Maybe," I told Ali, my tone attempting to hide my coldness. "Just let me know."

That summer one of my friends invited me to translate for his wife as she did her interview for US citizenship. He picked me up and we drove to Kansas City for the interview. We listened to Senegalese hip-hop on the way over. After being checked into the location, we waited in the lobby. After waiting in the lobby we were summoned in to the office. The questions were straightforward, wanting to make sure that she'd be a good citizen and do the country no harm. Did she have any family members that were terrorists? Did she have any family members that had given money to terrorists? Did she plan to pay her taxes? I struggled with the word for taxes, but we made it through.

That evening I returned to Ali's apartment for a haircut. Ideally, he would someday be going through those same interview questions to become an American citizen. And what would he do with his freedom? What was I doing with mine?

I returned to Ali's apartment for further haircuts. As it was getting colder, we set up the chair in the bathroom. He again turned on the music and the clippers. We were developing a routine, one that I had not had in years.

The previous two women I had gone to for haircuts did not share my Christian worldview. In college, sitting in the chair in her salon, she asked me what kind of a Christian I was. I used the word "evangelical" and all of a sudden everything got cold and heavy. Perhaps I should have said, "A good one— that's what type of Christian I am."

With Ali, while he cut my hair, I hoped that we shared a worldview, but I was too timid to prod. What business of mine was it if he was meeting girls at the swimming pool? Perhaps he was just more social than I was, and intending to marry. I may have been the small group leader, but was it my job to police his life? Still, I longed for him to long for what I longed for. Jesus. The good news permeating all of life and going out to the nations. Instead, it seemed he was trying to hide it and hush it up.

He finished up my haircut in the bathroom, and I swept up my hair with my hand and flushed it down the toilet.

That winter, there was a snowstorm so substantial that I didn't drive to church. This was a rarity for me. I never missed church. Not having WiFi in my house, I wasn't even able to stream the service. I did, however, receive a text from Ali. There would be an afternoon concert at Rose Music Hall, and he offered to pick me up. Just like he had for the opera. I said I'd go.

We stood inside the Rose Music Hall. I had not been here for years. My first memory of it was from high school, seeing the punk band Guttermouth. The singer was making politically incorrect statements from the stage, and eventually someone from the audience climbed onstage to take a swing at him. We were all shocked by the violence.

Today things were tamer. Ali recognized two girls in stocking caps near the front. We went up to say hi. One was a lawyer, who had helped him with something before.

The bluegrass/roots band played. The man playing bass was barefoot and wearing overalls. Every measure of the song he'd do a high kick to win over the crowd.

The band went into a cover of "Bitter Sweet Symphony", one of my favorite songs, and the title for the production company for the songs I myself was making. It came off almost as a hymn. I realized I had not sung or participated in music at church that morning, and this was a sort of secular supplement. It was like a small gift from God for the day.

After the concert Ali and I went out to the patio where opposing barriers had been set up for a snowball fight. We took spots side by side and took aim at the others on the other side of the patio. I had gloves on, Ali didn't. But that didn't slow his zeal and glee, chucking snowballs at the other side and dodging them on ours. He laughed and beamed. This was probably the healthiest thing we could do on a Sunday afternoon, after being cooped up all weekend. The adrenaline and endorphins were going.

I offered him my gloves on the way back to his car, but he said he'd be okay. That Sunday we may not have shared explicit worship for Christ, be we did share— or he was grooming me into— enjoyment of life.

Bike Trip

In 2018, my goal was to bike the Lewis and Clark Trail. I had been kicking it around in my head for all of one day —the day that I had pulled the bike out of the garage shed, skirting spider babies. It was like how in the midst of New Year's Resolutions men buy weightlifting gear for January 1, not having even been to the gym yet. In my case, I biked on flat tires to the bike shop, where they indulged me in a tire pump and alignment check. While I waited, I opened up a pamphlet for the Bike Across Missouri trip. *So it is possible*, I thought. Except in my case, I would be heading North and West, I imagined.

I likely got the idea for the trip from looking at a poem about Lewis & Clark I had written a year previous. I was now adapting curriculum to go along with it, to share with middle school students. I felt that living into the experience of Lewis & Clark would be a way to really integrate things, even if it meant biking almost 5,000 miles.

I then proceed to my dentist appointment, biking along the gravelly shoulder of Highway 63. I passed the wooden crucifixes where a few people had died in traffic accidents, then up the off-ramp to the dentist's office. I had called to warn them that I would be a little late. I did not mention how sweaty—it was late June—and stinky I would be. When I arrived, I offered to come back some other time, but the dental hygienist was ready to muddle through. I toweled off my arms with brown paper towels in the bathroom before hitting the chair.

That evening, I asked Dad to meet me in the driveway with his bike for an interview. I had a few interviews and podcasts in the works. Almost every friendship and interaction in my life I viewed as worthy of video adaptation, or at least podcast material. It was too small a thing for me to enjoy my own friends and life myself; I wanted to share it with the masses.

We stood next to our bikes, having positioned two iPhones on tripods to catch us from two oblique angles—like the cinematography in *Selma* when Martin Luther King Jr. is in jail.

"So I'm toying with an idea," I told Dad.

"Yeah?" he was still wearing his bike shorts from his ride home from work.

"What if I biked the Lewis & Clark trail?" I chuckled nervously.

"Well. That's certainly a doable thing," Dad said. It was along the lines of "you can be whatever you want to be when you grow up," though I was 32. Dad gave some further feedback.

"So first of all, I think if you build up yourself to a respectable distance every day, then that would be the gauge of how you can do this."

And that was all I needed—aside from a ride home in Dad's Prius— my bike loaded on the back.

I had the summer off. Not just because school was out of session. I had quit my job to start a writing and poetry ministry. I had not had any actual gigs yet, but I imagined touring all of Missouri to present a poetry workshop to middle school classrooms. Workshop was the word I was using, even though I didn't actually want to help kids write. I just wanted to share stuff I had been thinking about. The plan was to point to episodes in history where good stuff had happened. The abolition of the slave trade. Bonhoeffer resisting Hitler. Lewis and Clark exploring the Louisiana Purchase. Stuff that had already happened. You could call it good news. It was edutainment, in the words of the hip-hop group Boogie Down Productions. And my ministry would also implicitly point to the gospel—the good news of Jesus. I wouldn't have to actually say Jesus' name in a classroom. In fact, I would go out of my way to avoid it. It was enough that Bonhoeffer was a Christian, etc. All the students would have to do was a little tracing back for an encounter with Jesus.

The next day I woke up at 3:30am and started a poem about David Brainerd. The good news? Positive interactions between colonists and Native Americans. I realized I could use the same rhyme structure as my song about Dietrich Bonhoeffer— and just flip lines like a MadLib for the new subject matter.

Then at 6am I headed out to the trail. My older brother Stu once mentioned biking to Rocheport and back in a doable way, so I figured that'd be my goal for the day.

There was another couple on bikes when I neared the turn-off for Rocheport. They headed left, where there was a bathroom and water fountain. A shaded area with benches and map displays. I figured I just needed to turn right, so I kept going.

I biked past the cave areas, stopping to climb up the slopes a bit to get a closer look. The last time I had climbed up the side of a trail with a friend was with my friend Matt in Chattanooga. We were on our way up to Lookout Mountain, passing confederate monuments and people coming down the trail. When we reached the top of the mountain, Matt's phone had somehow switched into another language. I assumed it was Telegu, with Roman Script. This I took as a sort of transfiguration experience. Jesus takes his disciples up a mountain for a glimpse at his glory, and now I was being led up a mountain for a peek at my future. It was exactly the encouragement I needed for commencing with the multilingual musical phase of my life. There had to be something to it. Bringing people together by broadening their horizons.

I came to the beginnings of a winding switchback trail that would lead up to the *Les Bourgeois* winery. I parked my bike and helmet at the base, wondering if I should attempt to hide them more. But who would steal a bike on a trail? This was an opportunity to trust God, something I was trying to do in all of life.

I walked up the trail and made my way to the A-Frame dining area. It was closed today. I walked inside the restaurant where my friends had had their wedding reception years before. The restaurant was closed as well. Still, my mind was stirring, churning. I had plans for a monastic vows ceremony. I was not joining any particular religious order, just trying to celebrate being single. It would work well with traveling across Missouri in order to do the poetry workshops. I would be a troubadour evangelist.

I knew the building was officially closed this morning. But I picked up the business cards and moved a little closer to the kitchen where I overheard talking. Two women were laughing and preparing something. I apologized and introduced myself, and asked whom I would contact to see about renting the place out. One of the women directed me back towards the door and handed me a brochure that listed the rental options. It was going to be pricey. But it'd be worth it. I decided not to make any official decisions yet, but I would keep it in mind for when the time came to officially make the move.

I walked back down the switchback to my bike. No one had stolen it. Good. I could trust God. I could trust him with the minute. I could trust him with the seemingly extravagant— like a traveling poetry ministry, or a trip up the Lewis & Clark Trail.

I hopped on the bike to finish the last stretch to the town of Rocheport itself. My mind continued. I biked around downtown Rocheport for a while before heading up the hill to Highway BB. It was a steep climb so I put the bike in the lowest gear. But eventually I gave up and stepped off the bike to walk it. I knew that down the road towards the interstate there had once been an ice cream shop.

On the walk back, I remembered that one of my counselors had her practice in a home nearby. I had seen her for months at a time when she was in her Columbia location. I stopped seeing her for a while, only to realize that she had moved to a new location overlooking the Missouri River. I had a register of back payments I needed to make. At a time when I didn't have insurance to cover it, I asked if I could pay less than her standard hourly rate. She accepted, for a time, until her secretary informed me that she would be able to do so no longer.

When I received an inheritance from Grandma, I decided to try to make it up to my counselor. I wrote a letter to her and enclosed a check. I googled her new address and made my way out to the Rocheport location. Her office was in the basement of someone else's house. The owner of the house told me to go ahead and walk around to the back and enter in the basement. She would be there. I walked in and greeted her. She was sitting in her comfortable chair, just waiting, it seemed, to help set people free. She was happy to see me. I was there that day not because I needed counseling, but because I felt like I needed to thank her.

By the time I returned to deliver her the check in Rocheport, I was feeling much better. I did not want to have to return to counseling. I just wanted to return to let her know I was cured and to thank her. I recalled she appreciated it when people returned to thank her. She often never heard back, and didn't know exactly how people were doing once they stopped coming to counseling. I handed her the check and envelope and exited the door before she had a chance to open it.

A short time later she responded to me with a letter. She again thanked me for the funds and informed me that she had passed them on to a widow that she had been seeing in her practice.

And now, on my day of bike riding, I decided to swing by once again; a surprise visit. As I tried to remember which house it was, a gardener asked me if I knew what I was looking for.

"Does Marie still work here? The counselor?" I walked my bike up the gravel driveway, next to a farm-style fence made of linked timbers.

"She does. But she hasn't worked for a while. She's been having quite a few health complications," the man informed me. "She's pretty much trapped in bed."

"Oh that's rough. I was hoping to surprise her with a visit today." He paused for a moment. He pulled out his iPhone and dialed her. I stood a few feet away next to the fence until it was my turn to talk. There were apple trees nearby.

"Hi Marie," the man said. "I've got a man here who'd like to talk to you. He used to be one of your clients. I'll put him on. Here he is." He handed me the phone.

"Hi Marie, this is Scott. Scott Belden."

"Hi Scott. It's good to hear from you."

"Yeah, I was just going for a bike ride today and thought I'd swing by to surprise you."

"That's nice."

"Yeah, I just wanted to say thank you again. I was really depressed years ago and you did so much to just listen to me and help me."

"You're welcome. It is nice to hear from you."

I recalled that she had worked in a high school as a guidance counselor early in her career, but then switched to private practice, because of a concern that she could not share the gospel directly with students. It said so on her webpage bio for the counseling practice.

"I remember that you once said you liked working with high school students, but you didn't feel like you could stay as a counselor because you weren't allowed to share the gospel directly with them."

"That's right, that was how I felt."

"Well, I think I've figured out a way of how to do it." The implicit gospel.

"That's great," she said, probably not knowing exactly what I was talking about.

"In fact, I'm going to have an event. October 20th. If you can make it, I'd love to have you." It was the vows ceremony I had in the works, to kick off the ministry.

"Okay, October 20th, I'll see if I can make it."

"It will most likely be at *Les Bourgeois*, but I will let you know."

"Okay thank you, I am not really mobile nowadays, but I'll see what I can do." I imagined her arriving on the night of the celebration in a mobile bed, or with a walker. I would let Mom and Dad know that this was the woman who had helped cure me, against all odds.

It was going to be a long shot to try to bike the Lewis & Clark trail. Somehow I just needed to get back to Columbia. Biking closer to midday was much different from biking at 7am. The shade evaporated. I had to take frequent rest stops at the benches overlooking the Missouri River. It felt good to take my helmet off, to let the heat dissipate from my head. I had no water. I was going to be sunburned.

By the time I got back to the water fountains and the parking lot near the Rocheport turnoff, I knew that I was going to be very sore. I gulped water from the faucet for quite some time. Then I took off my shoes and socks and laid on the wooden benches. I was skinny enough to fit under the dividing wall of the bulletin board. I had lost a lot of weight since quitting my job at the high school. Normally I was 155, but I had shrunk to 137, then back to 143. This was Mr. Roger's weight. I felt that it was a good sign.

I did not have enough energy to make it back to Columbia. I would need to wait and depend on the mercy of anyone who had a vehicle and was headed back to town.

I laid on my back with my arms stretched out. The Jesus pose. This was easy, in a way. All I had to do was lay there. And if I died, I died.

Eventually a man did arrive. I noticed him putting his bike into the back of his pickup. I worked up the nerve to ask him if he was headed back to Columbia. Thankfully, he was. He let me ride with him.

"That's quite a bike ride," he remarked as I told him how far I had been. Especially as it was only my second day back into biking.

He dropped me off at my house. I looked at the clock on the stove and realized it was past noon. I had missed my daily prayer and Scripture readings for the day. Since I had so much time off in the summer, I had started reading the same passage in multiple languages at regular intervals during the day. 9am in English, 12pm in French, 3pm in Wolof, 6pm in Italian. As with my bike trip, I didn't know where it would lead. I was just going. I felt drawn in the direction of the poetry ministry and Lewis & Clark Trail, but did not realize how unfeasible it would be until later— later being the diagnosis of bipolar disorder.

One of my greatest pleasures in life has been the sense of being led by God. Some of my favorite hymns carried the theme— All the Way My Savior Leads Me, He Leadeth Me, etc. But what to do when I imagined I was being led by God, but was instead being led by misfires in my brain? How sovereign was God? Would he work all things together for good, including my goofy thinking? Preacher Charles Spurgeon was quoted as saying, "I believe that every particle of dust that dances in the sunbeam does not move an atom more or less than God wishes." What would he say of my bike trip? Was I somehow still in God's will?

At some level I assume God's will is for our healing, whether temporally or ultimately. He probably did not wish for me to remain in a confused and dangerous state. Counselors and others recognized this, and served as God's instruments in my life to bring me healing, even when my eyes wandered to the ends of the earth— or at least, Missouri.